How To Be A Class A Player

Alex Dunne

A Manual for Class B Players

Thinkers' Press 1987

First Edition: November 1987

ISBN: 0-938650-41-6

Request for permissions and republication rights should be addressed in writing to:

Thinkers' Press
331 Union Arcade Building
Davenport, IA 52801

DEDICATED TO:
Janet, who gives me peace and tranquility.

CONTENTS

INTRODUCTION

This book is written for the above average tournament chess player who would like to improve. This means you. As a Class B player you are already rated above 60% of the tournament players playing today. Your goal may be to become a Master; you might even have lesser ambitions to become at least an expert. But before you can attain either of these goals, you must first become a Class A player (Elo: 1800-1999). Later you may want to read *How To Become a Candidate Master* (Thinker's Press). Today you must learn how to play like and beat Class A players, for this is how you become a Class A player.

Roughly speaking, a Grandmaster is defined as a player who will score three out of five (or better) against Masters. A Master will score, roughly, three or more out of five against Experts, and an Expert will do the same in a field of Class A players. Right now in your tournament experience, you have probably noticed that you can handle the Class C players. They may give you a tussle, but your record against them is well on the positive side.

But then there are the Class A players. They are the sharks in your pool. Unless you are a very unusual Class B player, these minisharks are scoring 60% or more of the time against you.

There is a reason for this: Class A players play better chess than you do. It is the design of this book to reveal to you the difference in play between the Class A player and the Class B player to enable you to understand how to think and play Class A chess.

The typical chess book uses quite a different approach. Most books select Master games analysed by Masters in an attempt to raise the reader immediately to the Master level of play. For the somewhat above average player this is a long jump beyond Bob Beamon's. A journey of 1,000 miles must begin with a single step. Though these Master-level books contain beautiful, instructive, and entertaining games, and can be worthwhile to read, it is the belief of this author that these books need to be supplemented with a book like *How To Become a Class A Player.*

If you wish to improve your chess, you do not go out and challenge the World Champion to a match. Rather, you would find a player who is only a little better than you to play, and you would play him until you learned from him and beat him. That is the way to improve. This book will give you that opportunity. The games contained within are games between Class B players and Class A players. The games were selected from recent U.S. tournaments. In these games we shall see the typical strengths and weaknesses of the Class B player and will discuss how the Class A player, usually, takes advantage of them both.

When you play over these games, you will take the side of the Class A player. If you are going to learn to play like a Class A player, you may as well sit in his chair. A word of warning–you will not win every game from the Class A player's seat. No Class A player can so dominate Class B players just as no Class B player can expect 100% results against Class C players; there are lessons to be learned from losses and draws as well as wins.

One final word about studying these games. There are thirty-five chapters in this book, thirty-five tournament games. These games were played with a clock running, ticking away, adding extra pressure on the participants. It is one thing to study games in the quiet of your den. It is another thing, again, to play a tournament game. Since it is your intention, presumably, to be a Class A player in the tournament arena, not to be a Class A kibitzer, the best way to study this book is one (or possibly two) games a day, with a chess clock running by your side. Set your side of the clock for two hours for 40 moves. This time is recommended because you will find that since your opponent takes almost no time, you will not be able to think "on his time." Take a 3-by-5 index card to cover up the moves. A small rectangle can be cut out of the upper left hand side to reveal White's move and still cover up Black's response when you are "playing" the Black pieces.   Alex Dunne

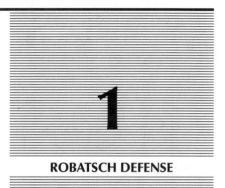

ROBATSCH DEFENSE

1. ROBATSCH DEFENSE
White: 1648 Player
Black: You

1. d4

By the time a player has achieved Class A strength, he usually has an opening repertoire. These openings do not always fit his style. As a Class A player (and you had better get used to that title as you will be called that from now on) you should have some openings you know fairly well. How do you develop this familiarity? One way is to buy a good book on the openings. *How To Be a Class A Player* will not comment extensively on opening play, for several reasons. One of these reasons is the Class A player needs to be able to apply general principles and specific calculations in his handling of the opening. Memorization of lines counteracts these chess strengths.

If your memory is excellent, go ahead and memorize lines. If your memory is good, poor, or indifferent, you will be much further ahead to learn the ideas behind the chess openings and proceed in your own direction. Later you can learn variations to the nth move.

1

In this game you will play a Robatsch (or Modern) Defense. Your plan is to fianchetto your King Bishop and play to fight for e5 and d4. Let us see how the Class A player proceeds logically.

1. ..., g6 2. e4 Bg7 3. Be3

This is a non-booked move. When a Class B player makes a non-book move, the Class A player should first look to see if he can refute it. On general principles, is there anything wrong with 3. Be3?

3. ..., c5!?

This is healthy, aggressive play. Black's other choice is 3. ..., Nf6 4. Nc3 d6 with normal play. Of the two choices, 3. ..., c5 is more apt to bring home a quick victory.

4. Nc3!?

This is well-played–the passive 4. c3 is not as good. To be a successful Class A player, an aggressive forwardgoing attitude is necessary.

4. ..., Nc6?!

This is an overplay. Black is pursuing his plan, the fight for d4, but he overlooks an important consideration–correct was 4. ..., cxd 5. Bxd4 Nf6 and if 6. Nd5 e6! 7. Nxf6+ Bxf6 8. Bxf6 Qxf6 and Black is at least equal.

5. d5?!

White, too, does not see Black's weakness. After 5. dxc! White has an extra Pawn which will put strong pressure on Black's game. Exactly what is happening here? The Class A player has a definite plan–fight to control d4.

The Class B player is responding to each Black move, counterpunching without a plan. Yes, there have been a few errors in the first five moves, but the player with the plan will usually dominate the counterpuncher.

5. ..., Nd4 6. N1e2 e5

Continuing his plan to control d4.

7. dxe

White, who does not have a plan, has no yardstick with which to measure his moves. Using Black's plan (control of d4) we can see that 7. dxe fits into Black's plan, not White's: after 7. ..., dxe, Black's Queen is "developed" and controls d4, plus White's Queen Pawn has moved three times to capture a Pawn that has moved only once. Black's game is healthy.

7. ..., dxe6 8. Bxd4?!

Lacking a plan, White seeks simplification in the center, but once again this only fits into Black's hand. Why?

8. ..., cxd4 9. Na4?

The Class B player would automatically reject 9. Nb1!? White's best try.

9. ..., Qa5+ 10. c3 (1)

10. ..., Bd7!

The Class A player wants to play "cleanly." To pursue the Knight heavily by 10. ..., b5!? allows 11. Nxd4! bxa4 12. Bb5+ Kf8 (Why not 12. ..., Bd7 ? Analyse!) 13. 0-0 and White will have two Pawns for the piece and some attacking

chances. By developing with threats, Black will soon have a stronger game.

11. b3 Bxa4 12. bxa4 Rd8

Black follows elementary principles (development, center control) and White's game is in ruins. Though material is even, White's game is extremely difficult. How did this happen so fast?

13. Qb3 d3 14. Nd4

White tosses a Knight into the pot in order to play on for a while. It now becomes the *duty* of the Class A player to win as cleanly and efficiently as possible, otherwise White might organize a defense of sorts.

14. ..., Bxd4 15. Kd2 Qg5+ 16. Kd1 Bxf2 17. c4 Qe3 18. Qb5+ Rd7 19. Qb4 (2)

For the moment, White has contained Black's threats. Now Black should make plans to end the game. Do not move the chess pieces on the board. What is Black's clearest winning line?

19. ..., Nf6

If you visualized the plan of ..., Nf6; ..., Ne4; ..., Bh4 and

4

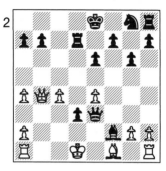

..., Nf2+ you have the killer instinct. When the King is in a mess, think checkmate.

20. c5 Nxe4 21. c6 Rd4

This will win in short order, but 21. ..., bxc 22. Qb8+ Rd8 23. Qb4 Bh4 is more logical.

22. c7 Rc4 23. Qb5+ Ke7 White Resigns

What can you learn from this game? Errors, especially in the opening, are common, but the player who has a clear-cut, simple plan (control of d4) will usually come out of the opening in better shape. Playing planlessly (just develop and see what happens) will usually come to grief.

2. ENGLISH OPENING
White: You
Black: 1654 Player

1. c4

There is a school of thought that says until you reach Class A strength, 1. e4 is the best opening for White. The idea is that before you can play positional chess, you must first know tactics. This is sound advice, but now that you are a Class A player (or on your way to becoming one) you can try your hand at slower openings. There are many nuances in playing these openings that Class A players (and experts) will not understand. This is OK. Your Class B opponent is even less likely to understand them.

1. ..., Nf6 2. Nf3 e6 3. g3 c5 4. Bg2 Nc6 5. 0-0 a6?!

Up to this point your opponent has played solid moves. You should now consider 5. ..., a6. What action should White take now? What is your plan?

6. d4

If you decided ..., a6 was a waste of time and now you should open up the center, your planning is correct. When your opponent falls behind in development, you need to open up lines.

6. ..., d5 (3)

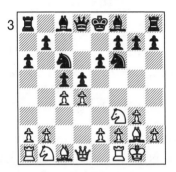

This is a complicated opening position and the Class A player may well find calculating the variations impossible. This is where the Class A player should show his superiority by a better grasp of opening principles. What is your plan now?

7. cxd5 Nxd5 8. dxc5?!

Class A players slip too. The opening is not always easy to play. White has made solid, healthy developing moves. There is truth in chess: White should play 8. Nc3 as 8. ..., cxd4 9. Nxd5 Qxd5 is met by 10. Nxd4! with a strong game for White. The Class A player in this game doesn't see this. That's OK. But he should plan to use his center. OK for White is 8. e4 Nc7 9. dxc with a slight advantage. The text develops Black.

8. ..., Bxc5 9. Qc2 Qb6 10. Nc3 Nxc3 11. bxc3?!

White willingly takes on a Pawn weakness and the advantage of the opening tips in Black's favor. After 11.

Qxc3 White's game is still healthy. Why is the c-Pawn weak? The Class A player knows that after ..., Bd7 and ..., Rc8 the c-Pawn will come under pressure, but he wants to avoid 11. Qxc3 Nd4 12. Nxd4 Bxd4 13. Qa3 Bc5 14. Qc3 Bd4 etc. White's choice is practical–he avoids the draw against his lower rated opponent even at the cost of a weakness. The odds are in his favor even if the position isn't.

11. ..., Ne7?!

Black is afraid to castle–11. ..., 0-0 12. Ng5 g6 13. Ne4 Be7 14. Bh6 when White has some attacking chances. But, notice his plan: he is only using the pieces he already has developed. The Class A player would not play this way. He would try to further his game, probably playing ..., e5 or even 11. ..., 0-0 12. Ng5 f5 with counterplay.

12. Ng5 Ng6 13. h4

White is intent on attack, even if he disturbs his King's position. This aggression will usually pay off against Class B players *and* other Class A players, too. Against an Expert or Master it will cost dearly. Is 13. h4 a weak or a strong move? How strong is your opponent?

13. ..., h6 14. Ne4 Qa5 15. a4

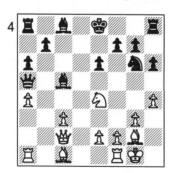

This is sometimes called *coffee house* chess–15. ..., 0-0 16. Nxc5 Qxc5 17. Ba3 wins an exchange. Why coffee house? Because White had a better way–15. Nxc5 Qxc5 16. a4 and Black will soon be unable to castle and White will have two strong Bishops. Black's best play now is 15. ..., Be7 with only a tiny edge for Black.

15. ..., Bb6?

Why does Black blunder here? He blunders because he lacks a defensive plan. He has been responding to White's threats move by move, and this is a poor way to play chess.

16. Nd6+

Analyse why Black loses decisive material after 16. ..., Ke7 or 16. ..., Kf8.

16. ..., Kd7

Of course, 16. ...,Kf8 17. Nc4! is destruction. Now even worse happens.

17. Nxf7 Rf8 18. Qxg6 Qxc3

Black is playing on reflex. The Class A player's job is now to win smoothly, giving Black no counterchances.

19. Ba3 Bxf2+ 20. Kh1

Avoiding all traps.

20. ..., Bc5 21. Bxc5 Black Resigns

After 21. ..., Qxc5 22. Rad1+ Ke7 23. Qxg7 Black's game is *kaput.* The lesson to be learned: constant pressure will usually break your opponent.

3. ROBATSCH DEFENSE
White: 1634 player
Black: You

1. e4

By now you should be getting the idea that as a Class A player, you can beat these Class B players. This is the proper attitude! How does one develop this attitude? The best way is through success–in consistently (or nearly so) beating the Class B players. This is your goal: Beat White!

1. ..., d6 2. d4 Nf6 3. Nd2

Whoops–though this has been played before, the Class A player recognizes it as an unusual, somewhat passive, play. You should analyse the position now (Yes, already on Move 3!) to convince yourself you cannot immediately take advantage of White's position. How do you continue?

3. ..., g6

10

Black plays correctly. Continuing the Robatsch formation is a good Black strategy.

4. N1f3 Bg7 5. c3 0-0 6. Bd3 Nc6 7. 0-0 Nd7!

Upon checking an opening book, *ECO* (Encyclopedia
of Chess Openings) we find 7. ..., Nd7! is a recommenda-
tion of GM Parma. Anderson-Hartston, Hastings 1972-3
continued 7. ..., e5?! What does this tell the Class A player?
It should do two things. One, it should give him confidence
in handling this opening, and two, it will always help the
Class A# player to improve his game by checking his opening play against "book"–Master play. In this case, the Class
A player has improved on Master play to this point. This
is rare, but it does happen. What is Black's plan?

8. Re1 e5 9. d5

White decides that 9. dxe N7xe5 10. Nxe5 Nxe5 11.
Bc2 d5! 12. f4 Bg4 is not a position he would care to play
and so locks the center.

9. ..., Ne7 (5)

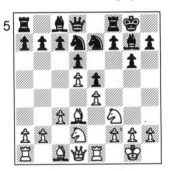

10. Nb3

This is typical of Class B play–White wants to develop
his Queen Bishop so he moves the Knight away. He should

instead have a plan-queenside play. For this reason 10. c4 followed possibly by b4, Nb3 and c5 should be White's intentions. Black, on the other hand, has more aggressive ideas. What should Black's plan be?

10. ..., f5 11. Ng5?!

Why is this move weak?

11. ..., Nf6 12. exf gxf 13. Ne6?!

This type of play can be very annoying in a King's Indian formation (Pawn on c4, Knight on c3) but here it is out of place. White could wait until Black further weakened his position by ..., h6 before leaping in–13. c4!? but Black already has a good game. As Class A players realize, the player with the better opening usually has the better chances.

13. ..., Bxe6 14. dxe6 e4 15. Bc2 Qc8

Taking dead bead on the advanced Pawn. Once this Pawn falls, Black will have fine chances.

16. Nd4 a6

Careful play–Black could also play directly 16. ..., c5 17. Nb5 d5 and the e-Pawn dies.

17. f3 c5 18. Nb3 Qxe6 19. fxe fxe 20. Bxe4?!

A faulty combination that the Class A player refutes nicely. Plan Black's refutation. If you have difficulty in analyzing ahead, one method to improve your ability to calculate is to take the "White To Move and Win" problems published in magazines like *Chess Life* or *Chess Correspondent.* Try to solve the problem. If you succeed, good! If you don't, go over the solution "in your head." Don't touch the chess pieces. Then go back to the board and try to visualize the solution. Practice in this fashion will improve your ability to calculate.

20. ..., Nxe4 21. Qc2 (6)

21. ..., Qf5!

If you selected 21. ..., d5 22. Nxc5 Qc6 23. Nxe4 dxe4 24. Rxe4, you would still be winning but you would have a long and difficult struggle ahead of you. Set the position back to Move 20. Try visualizing the more efficient way to win.

22. Qxe4 Qf2+ White Resigns

Black played this game very well. Class A players should strive not only to win, but to play well. An esthetically pleasing game is a sign your chess is improving.

4. COLLE OPENING
White: You
Black: 1654 Player

1. d4 d5 2. e3

This move hails the Colle Opening. It is an ideal Class A opening. The Colle has a clear-cut plan. White plans to follow up with Bd3, Nf3, N1d2, c3, 0-0 and then either Re1 or e4 directly, opening up the center with fine attacking chances. The Colle isn't seen too much in Master chess in the 1980's because it is too easy for a Master playing Black to equalize. For this reason the Colle isn't good against top-flight (Expert +) competition, but it can be a Class B killer.

2. ..., Nf6 3. Bd3 e6 4. N1d2 c5 5. c3 (7)

5. ..., c4?!

This is an important point of the game. We do not like to be dogmatic, but it is almost always bad to play ..., c4 early in a Colle Opening. The Class A player should know why and how to take advantage of it. Why? and how? Answer these two questions before proceeding.

14

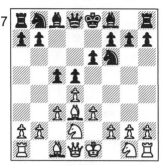

6. Bc2

The correct retreat: White plans to enforce e4. Black may find it embarassing to allow e4-e5 gaining central territory, and after ..., dxe, Nxe4 the Pawn on c4 may well prove weak, and White has central pressure. This central pressure is key to White's attacking chances.

6. ..., g6?!

Black is showing unfamiliarity with opening principles– having established a path for his Bishop (f8 to a3) Black should use this path and thus save time. (Make piece moves, not Pawn moves!) Better was 6. ..., Be7. Why not 6. ..., Bd6? This is OK, too, if Black plans to meet e4 with ... dxe4, else e5 would fork Bishop and Knight.

7. f4

This does not quite fit in with the Colle system idea. White could play 7. e4 immediately, or delay it (probably better–the idea that the threat is stronger than the execution is true in chess, too). After 7. Nlf3 Bg7 8. 0-0 0-0 9. e4 dxe4 10. Nxe4 Nxe4 11. Bxe4 Nc6 12. Qe2 with advantage to White. Still, White's idea is aggressive. He plans Nlf3, 0-0, and Ne5 with some attacking chances.

7. ..., b5?! (8)

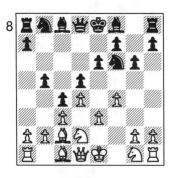

Premature. Having prepared to fianchetto his Bishop (6. ..., g6?!) Black should continue with 7. ..., Bg7. The Class A player knows to make necessary moves first. Now, plan to take advantage of ..., b5.

8. a4!?

Bravo! The Class A player is not inflexible. Though he had plans to invade the center by Ne5, etc., he can adjust to the position on the board. This Pawn formation (White: a2,b2,c3,d4/ Black: a7,b5,c4,d5) is one Class A players must be familiar with.

If White had continued with 8. e4, then 8. ..., dxe4! 9. Nxe4 Bb7 and Black has some fighting chances. Now the Bishop will be deflected from g7.

8. ..., b4 9. cxb4 Bxb4 10. Nf3 Nc6 11. 0-0 0-0 12. Ne5

The result of Black's misplays on Moves 5-7 becomes apparent. Black's kingside has a large hole in it and White's pieces will soon be visiting. The Class A player's job is to visualize in general terms how White will conduct his kingside attack. How will he do this?

12. ..., Ne7

Trying to bring another piece over to defend his King,

16

but better was to plan a longer-range defense based on occupation of e4, the critical square in the center. Study the position after 12. .., Bxd2! 13. Bxd2 Nxe5 14. fxe5 Ne4 15. Bxe4 dxe4 and note that Black has strengthened his chances to survive by simplification and center play. This is high-class Class A play. It is *planning* not *reacting*. 12. ..., Bxd2! is part of a defensive plan while 12. ..., Ne7 is just a reaction ("I'd better get another piece over there to defend my King.")

13. g4!

White's attack grows in strength. Notice White's formation, supported by the strong Knight on e5.

13. ..., Bb7 14. Qf3

The Class A player can usually attack well–here the Queen not only comes into attacking range of the Black King, but it protects the sensitive e4 square. Also good was 14. g5 locking on to the sensitive dark squares (as Black's Bishop is misplaced, remember?) There is another threat, too. What is it?

14. ..., Nd7?! 15. N2xc4! (9)

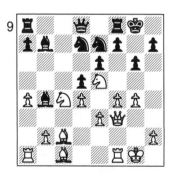

This pockets a Pawn, but you have to read the complications very carefully. Analyse the position. Note how far ahead you see after 15. ..., Qc7

15. ..., Qc7

The position is complicated. White needs to play in such a way as to clear things up.

16. Nxd7! dxc4 17. Nf6+ Kg7 18. Qh3!?

Commendable vitality! How far were you able to calculate? If you saw up to 17. Nf6+, you should force yourself to look farther. If you saw 18. Be4! your tactics are excellent–you should be a Class A player in no time. If you saw 18. Qh3!? Kxf6 that Black's King would come out to the center and be dangerously exposed, this is good chess thinking, but it is not calculation. The Class A player must learn to calculate.

18. ..., Rh8?!

You may not have been able to analyse 18. ..., Kxf6 19. Qxh7! Nd5 20. Bxg6! Ke7! 21. f5! with excellent attacking chances, but neither could your opponent. The Class B player violates an important rule of sacrifices–if you can't see why you can't take an opponent's piece, take it! Black might have been able to turn the game around. Instead he only thinks defense, and a poor defense at that.

19. g5 Qc6?

What's White's best move now? What was Black's best move? Why does Black overlook mate in one? Partly because it is tiring to defend throughout the game, partly because it is more fun to attack rather than defend. Black should have played 19. ..., h5. Once again, as usual, the attacker is rewarded.

20. Qh6 mate

5. SICILIAN DEFENSE
White: You
Black: 1670 player

1. e4 c5 2. Nf3 Nc6 3. d4 cxd 4. Nxd4 Nf6 5. Nc3 g6

The Dragon Variation of the Sicilian is another good line for Class A players playing a higher-rated opponent. The attacking motifs are fairly clear, making it easy to plan ahead. The two drawbacks to the Dragon are 1) It is extensively analysed, requiring an encyclopedic knowledge to play it correctly. The Class A player should study the Dragon closely if he wants to play it. This makes it an ideal line to play by correspondence, giving the Class A player plenty of time to explore the many crucial variations. 2) It is very complex—sacrificial combinations abound. The Class A player's tactics are usually better than the Class B's, but the Class A player's superiority lies in his better understanding of positional chess, not tactics. The Class B player's choice is correct in playing this line against you. It is one of his best chances for an upset.

6. Be3 Bg7 7. Be2

The Class A player should be familiar with the lines evolving from 7. Nxc6 if only to see if he would like to play them.

7. ..., 0-0 8. Qd2?! (10)

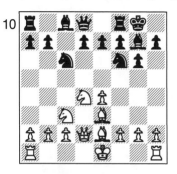

This is an error, but not one that is easy to see. Correct is 8. 0-0 but you need not worry if you selected 8. Qd2 as your move, too. It is easy to criticize this move at a desk, with an opening book available. In the heat of the game against a lesser-rated opponent, it is OK–*for this game only.* This is why the student who wishes to improve must study his own games. He must learn from his errors so he will not repeat them and can punish another player who makes the same error. Black can get a fine game now, if his memory is good, by 8. ..., d5 9. exd5 Nxd5 10. Nxd5 Nxd4 11. Bxd4 Qxd5 12. Bxg7 Qxg2! Crepeaux-Glatmann, Varna 1972. How can the Class A player find the move (8. ..., d5) without benefit of memory? He knows the general principles that if Black can play ..., d5 successfully in the Sicilian, he usually gets at least an equal game.

8. ..., Qb6?!

This cannot be a good move. White has three (or four) moves to consider. What are they? The Class A player should consider 9. Nb3, 9. 0-0-0, and 9. Ne6 (or 9. Nf5) How does he choose which one to play? After 9. Nb3 Qd8

21

10. 0-0-0 White has a healthy two tempi to begin his kingside attack. If 9. 0-0-0 Nxd4 10. Bxd4 Qc6 11. e5 Ne8 12. Bf3 White has all the chances. So what of 9. Ne6 (or 9. Nf5)? The Class A player will play this move only if he can analyse winning chances. So, analyse 9. Ne6. Is it playable? Does it win? Do not move the pieces on the board; move them in your head only.

9. Ne6?! Qxb2 10. Rb1 Nxe4!

This was the key move you had to foresee. What does White do now?

11. Rxb2 Nxd2?!

Did you analyse 11. ..., Bxc3 ? You should have. If not, do it now. Do you see that Black is OK?– 12. Qxc3 (analyse 12. Nxf8 Nxd2!) Nxc3 13. Nxf8 Kxf8 14. Bf3 Na4. This means that White didn't properly analyse 9. Ne6, that 9. Nb3 or 9. 0-0-0 were superior. But Black has to find the correct moves to achieve an equal position. The virtue of 9. Ne6 is that it is forward going–attacking, putting Black on his mettle. Go back to Move 9. Reanalyse 9. Ne6. See if you can follow the combination through after 11. ..., Bxc3.

12. Nxg7 Kxg7 13. Bxd2 (11)

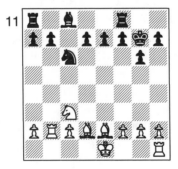

The flurry is over. White is a piece ahead for two

Pawns and has a considerable lead in development. The Class A player should expect to win here.

13. ..., d6 14. 0-0 Bf5 15. Bd3

White follows a plan of simplification by exchanging. Black's Bishop is active, White's passive. The exchange also takes the c-Pawn off the open file. Good play.

15. ..., Bxd3 16. cxd3 b6 17. Nd5 e6 18. Bc3+

Notice how the Class A player uses his active pieces: no abject retreat by 18. Ne3 here. Analyse how 18. ..., f6 is punished.

18. ..., e5 19. Rc1 Rac8 20. R2c2

The only open file is the c-file. You wouldn't mind exchanging a Rook or two to reach a winning ending.

20. ..., Nd8? Black Resigns

Difficult positions are easy to blunder in. Black resigned before you can play what killing move? The reason the Class B player lost this game is a lesser command of analysing combinations. This skill can be improved by you, if you work at it.

6. EVANS GAMBIT
White: 1641 Player
Black: You

1. e4 e5 2. Nf3 Nc6 3. Bc4 Bc5 4. b4

The Evans Gambit was popular over a century ago, but it has faded into near obscurity after Emanuel Lasker showed how to take its bite away in a famous game just before the turn of the century. So much for history. Here it is back, facing you in a tournament game. What do *you* do?

4. ..., Bxb4

Class A players should accept gambits offered by Class B players. After all, you are the better player. You now have a Pawn and the Class B player has to prove you wrong.

5. c3 Ba5 6. d4 d6!

Here is where knowledge counts. Lasker's recipe for taming the Evans Gambit was to allow White to regain the

Pawn–at a cost of a weakened Pawn structure. For example, 7. dxe5 dxe5 8. Qxd8+ Nxd8! 9. Nxe5 Be6 with a slight edge. The Class A player knows he should keep his position healthy, and it would be worth your while noticing the simplicity and depth of Lasker's plan. White wants to attack (hence the gambit). Black has allowed the regaining of the Pawn, but the Queens have been exchanged and White's Pawn structure is inferior. Solid opening play as Black! The Class A player who knows this opening idea need never fear an Evans Gambit.

7. Qb3 Qd7 (12)

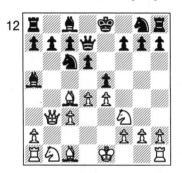

Again, knowledge of the openings is a powerful weapon. The player who is well-prepared in the opening has the advantage over the player who is ignorant. Though this move looks ugly, it is a well-conceived plan. Inferior is 7. ..., Qf6? 8. d5 winning a piece; playable, though, is 7. ..., Qe7 8. d5 Nd4! 9. Nxd4 exd4 10. Qa4+ Bd7 11 Qxa5 Qxe4+ 12. Kf1 d3 13. Nd2 Qe2+ 14. Kg1 Qe1+ 15. Nf1 d2 with advantage to Black. So why does Black not play 7. ..., Qe7 which looks more natural? Because 9. Qa4+ Qd7 10. Qxa5 b6 11. Nxd4! leads to an edge for White. It is not likely the Class A player could figure this out over the board. Study of the opening gives 7. ..., Qd7 as the right move.

How does a player who wants to be Class A strength study the openings? Correspondence play, as we have mentioned, is the best way. Study of your tournament games and books on how to play the opening are two other excellent alternatives.

8. 0-0

After 8. dxe5, Black should play the Lasker plan–8. ..., Bb6! 9. 0-0 Na5 with an advantage. This position, too, is worth studying for its general opening ideas.

8. ..., Bb6 9. Bb5 a6 10. Ba4

White wastes a tempo here and is nicely punished.

10. ..., Ba7!

Black has played the opening superbly and has gained the advantage. Prove to yourself that 11. d5 is weak for White. White's attack is almost non-existant. If you can play this well, you need to consider being an Expert, not a Class A player. Such is the power of knowledge. Now the game leaves the opening stage. We will watch how the Class A player uses his opening edge.

11. Bxc6 Qxc6 12. dxe5 Be6

Always sharp! Note Black's advantages here. What are they?

13. Qc2 0-0-0 (13)

14. Ng5?!

This is a typical Class B error. Black is almost fully developed–White's queenside is featherbedding. White should have tried 14. Ba3, developing, when 14. ..., d5! gives Black only a slight edge. Now you need to punish 14.

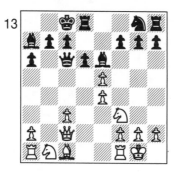

Ng5. What is your plan?

14. ..., dxe

Of course–this simple move gives Black a big edge: a Pawn plus, the open d-file, a sound Pawn structure (15. Nxe6 Qxe6). Black is winning.

15. Nd2 f6 16. Nxe6 Qxe6 17. Ba3

Now White is fully developed and Black needs to plan what to do with his Knight. Where does it go?

17. ..., Nh6?!

Better was the plan 17. ..., Ne7 ..., Ng6 ..., Nf4 with an attack, or 17. ..., Ne7 ..., Nc6 for defense. Black shouldn't mind the swap 18. Bxe7 Qxe7 as he is a Pawn ahead (swapping toward the endgame) and Black's Bishop is equal or better than White's Knight. On h6, the Knight's options are more limited.

18. Rab1 Rd7 19. Nb3 b6?! (14)

Black has played the opening like a Master; he is now playing the middle game like a Class C player. Class A players know the general rule–don't weaken the kingfield. This general principle should be broken only in extreme

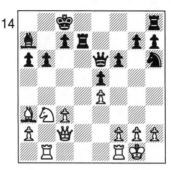

circumstances. By keeping his aggressive attitude, Black should have found 19. ..., Rhd8 20. Na5 Rd2 (Black could now play 20. ..., b5, too–note the difference!) 21. Qa4 b5 22. Qb4 Ng4 and Black's attack is dynamite.

Class A players need to seek out aggressive continuations. This is what makes them Class A players.

20. Qb2?!

After 20. Qe2! b5 21. Rfc1 Ng4 22. c4! Black is in trouble–22. ..., Nxf2 23. Bc5!

20. ..., Qc6 21. h3?

This hands the initiative right back to Black. What is White's best try? If you have doubts, check the note above.

21. ..., Rd3 22. Qe2 R8d8 23. Bc1 b5

Black frees his Bishop and all Black's forces (except his dumb Knight) are well-placed. You should expect to win shortly. What is your plan?

24. Bd2 Nf7 25. c4 bxc4 26. Na5 Qe6
27. Be3 Bxe3 28. fxe3 Rd2

Black is willing to exchange Queens as the ending

would be painful for White.

29. Qe1 Ng5 White Resigns (15)

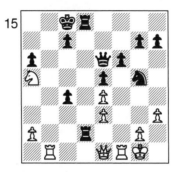

White gives up here, but you should verify the resignation. What is Black's clear-cut winning idea? The attack against White's King just fails as the pieces are set up now, but after 30. ..., Nxe4 31. a4 Qd5! 32. Nb7 Nc3 White's position falls completely apart.

This game demonstrates that though thorough knowledge of the opening is valuable, it is not enough. The middle game must also be played well. Some players forget this, believing the opening is all important. Notice how with just two moves, 17. ..., Nh6 and 19. ..., b6, White had his chances to come back into the game. A Class A player might well have taken advantage of these slips. He is always looking to attack. The Class B player is not usually so aggressive.

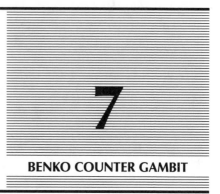
7. BENKO COUNTER GAMBIT
White: 1625 Player
Black: You

1. d4 Nf6 2. c4 c5 3. d5 b5 (16)

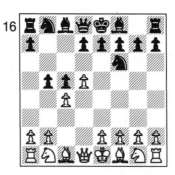

Most tournament players are familiar with the Benko Counter Gambit's ideas: Black sacrifices a Pawn on the queenside for development and open files to pressure White's queenside. Because of its clear-cut strategical ideas, it is a good line for Class A players to use against Class B players, especially as the Class B's defensive skills will not usually be up to defending his queenside.

4. b3

This is a typical reaction of a Class B player–he avoids the commitment, declining the gambit in favor of "safety." You will seldom see the Benko treated this way in upper levels of play. There White will take the Pawn (usually) and make Black prove the gambit's soundness. By adapting a passive stance, White presents Black with an easy development, but the game enters different channels of play.

4. ..., bxc4 5. bxc4 g6 6. Nc3 d6 7. e4

This is better than 7. Bb2 Bg7 8. f3 N8d7 9. e4 Rb8 with advantage to Black, *Masera-Benko, Reggio Emilia 1970-1.*

7. ..., Bg7 8. Rb1

The Class B player knows how to occupy open lines, too.

8. ..., N8d7 9. Bd3 0-0 10. N1e2 Ne5 11. 0-0

The Class B player is playing a Class A game. Black needs a plan at this time. What is a good plan?

11. ..., Ba6

Black's plan is to pressure c4. This plan is OK if followed through, but more productive might have been 11. ..., e6. Nevertheless, Black has started with an idea.

12. Nb5 (17)

12. ..., Nxd3?!

This is an important error and a position the Class A player should study. The move is an error for two reasons.

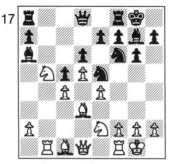

Black has started a plan–pressuring White's weakness, the c4 square. Though the exchange removes a defender, it also removes an attacker and brings out a new White piece that also defends c4. Black should have found 12. ..., Rb8 as 13. Nxa7 could be met by 13. ..., Rxb1 14. Bxb1 Qb8! 15. Nb5 Nxc4 with a superior game for Black.–Black's plan of pressuring c4 pays dividends.

Second: One of the toughest problems for the Class A player to solve (and one treated in the next volume in this series, *How To Become a Candidate Master*) is when to play for the two Bishops. In general, when the Pawns are locked, as here, the Knight is a slight favorite. Another way of looking at it is the Bishop on d3 has no moves but to retreat to c2, and here it would drop the c4 Pawn. Black's Knight on e5 can advance–Ng4, Nf3+, Nxd3, Nxc4 or retreat to d7 to go to b6 to further pressure White's c4. This makes the Knight a much better piece, now, than the Bishop, and the exchange is not in Black's favor. Notice, too, the exchange further develops White's game. This can only help the Class B player.

13. Qxd3 Nd7 14. a4 Nb6 15. Qb3 Bc8

Black sees his plan to attack c4 is doomed (12. ..., Nxd3?!) and switches his Bishop to another sector. What is Black's plan?

16. Bb2 e5?! (18)

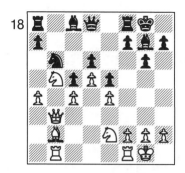

Here it is again. The Class A player knows the two Bishops constitute an advantage–he's heard it and read it plenty of times so he plays to preserve his two bums. This play is all right–if he has prepared to meet a5. Otherwise he is playing like a Class B player – just reacting to his opponent's threats and not really playing with a plan. Analyse the position after 16. ..., e5 17. a5.

17. a5 Nd7

If you analysed the position after 17. ..., Nd7 you would come to the conclusion that Black has a bad game. Black should have done that before 16. ..., e5. If he had, he would be thinking instead of just moving. Many a game is spoiled by just moving.

18. Nxd6 Rb8 19. Qa2 Nf6 20. Nxc8

And so Black loses the two Bishops anyway, and White is left with a strong passed d-Pawn.

20. ..., Nxe4!?

Black is desperate here and so he enters into unclear complications. This is a good gamble as otherwise White has a winning position. When should a player "gamble" and enter unclear complications? When there seems to be no better try. Here the gamble is worthwhile, else, Black loses another Pawn.

21. Nxa7 Nd2 22. Nc6 Rxb2?!

Surprise moves can be very nerve-wracking to an opponent, and excitable players can be overwhelmed by unexpected sacrifices in an "exciting" position. The Class A player does not want to play these (unsound) "surprise" moves, but he should be aware in desperate positions they sometimes work.

23. Qxb2?!

Black can give up on 23. Rxb2.

23. ..., Qg5 24. a6?!

With 24. f4! White could expect a resignation in a move or so.

24. ..., Nxc4 25. Qb7

When a Class B player has a clear-cut winning plan, he will go for it. Black is clearly lost.

25. ..., Nd2 26. a7 NxR/b 27. Rxb1 Qd2 Black Resigns

Black resigns rather than face a8(Q). Why did the Class A player lose this game? One–his Class B opponent played well. This will happen. Class B players can play a good game! Two–at the critical junction (Move 16), Black played without a plan. This kind of reactive play is a holdover from earlier days–your opponent makes a threat and you guard: no plan, just reaction. Such play should be avoided to play like a Class A player.

8. ENGLISH OPENING
White: 1743 Player
Black: You

1. c4 c5

Bobby Fischer once commented about playing Black–before you can start to play for a win, you must first obtain an equal game. Here 1. ..., c5 is probably as good as any play to achieve equality. The Class A player, however, is playing his natural prey, the Class B player. We saw in the previous game that the hunter can sometimes become the hunted. Sound, solid chess will defeat the Class B player.

2. Nc3 Nc6 3. g3 g6 4. Bg2 Bg7 5. e3 (19)

5. ..., d6

White has announced his intentions of playing d4 with his last move. The Class A player should make long range plans of how to treat this. He knows that after d4, he will probably play ..., cxd4. White will most likely reply exd4. Black would then like to be able to play ..., d5 so Black's best plan seems 5. ..., e6 6. Nle2 Nf6 7. 0-0 0-0 8. d4 cxd4 9. exd4 d5, with equality. The Class A player

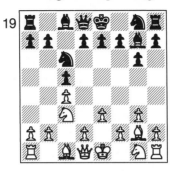

should know how to read Pawn structure to make his future plans.

6. N1e2 Nf6 7. 0-0 Bf5

An ambitious plan (it is good for a Class A player to be ambitious) to provoke e4, but Black is better off castling (make necessary moves first).

8. d4 0-0 9. e4 Bg4 10. f3

The Class B player fails to see the advantage of 10. d5 Nd4 11. f3 Nxe2+ 12. Qxe2 with advantage to White.

10. ..., cxd4 (20)

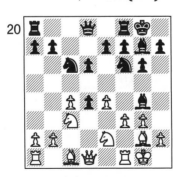

11. Nd5?!

And unable to read the complications after 11. Nxd4

Nxe4?! 12. Nxc6 Nxc3 13. Nxd8 Nxd1 14. fxg4! (not 14. Rxd1 Bc8! with an advantage) Bd4+ 15. Kh1 Nf2+ 16. Rxf2 Bxf2 17. Nxb7 Rab8 18. Na5 with winning chances, the Class B player selects a "safer" line. Here is where the Class A player has his edge–his ability to calculate. Turn the board around. Practice your ability to calculate. Confirm for yourself (without moving the pieces) that 11. Nxd4 Nxe4?! is good for White. Think it out!

11. ..., Be6 12. Kh1

White has difficulties in regaining the Pawn on d4 so he temporizes. This, too, is typical of the Class B player. White should take immediate steps to win the Pawn back, say by 12. Rb1 to force Black to commit himself. If Black is allowed to do as he pleases, he will be a Pawn ahead with a healthy game. Class A players prefer to be active.

12. ..., Qd7 13. N2f4 Bxd5

Black willingly gives the Pawn back in order to play in the center. This is not bad play. Master play might continue 13. ..., Nd8!? to hold on to the d-Pawn, but this is good Class A play.

14. exd5?

And weak Class B chess. White, happy to get his Pawn back, does not see Black's tactics. Correct was 14. cxd5. Analyse Black's plan now.

14. ..., Ne5 15. Qxd4 (21)

15. ..., Qc7!

Black wins a Pawn. Why is this move better than ..., Rfc8?

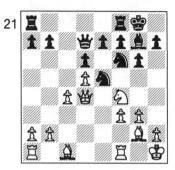

16. b3?! Nxf3! 17. Qf2

Too late White sees the X-ray attack on his Queen and Rook. Now he retreats, but his game is ruined.

17. ..., Nxh2! 18. Bb2 Nfg4
19. Qe2 Nxf1 20. Rxf1 Bxb2 21. Qxg4

White can't capture on b2 as ..., Ne3 simplifies even more.

21. ..., Rac8 22. Be4 (22)

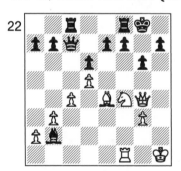

White is lining up his pieces for an attack. Notice how the Class A player calmly simplifies, breaking the attack using his large material advantage.

22. ..., f5 23. Qe2 fxe4 24. Qxb2 Qd7

Avoiding greed by 24. ..., g5 25. Ne6 Rxf1+ 26. Kg2 Rf7 27. Nxc7 and White still has chances to resist.

25. Kg2 Qf5 26. Rf2 a6

Black's advantage won't run away–he threatens ..., b5 opening up lines for his Queen Rook. Black's play is, as noticed, calm and solid.

27. Ne6 Qxf2+ 28. Qxf2 Rxf2+ 29. Kxf2 b5 White Resigns

There are many lessons to be learned from this game. Black played solid Class A chess, in the center, keeping the integrity of his position, refraining from making weakening moves. The Class B player who aspires to move up in the rankings should learn from this solidity. It makes a player very hard to beat and the steady pressure Black applied will eventually destroy almost any Class B player.

CENTER GAME

9. CENTER GAME
White: You
Black: 1615 Player

1. e4 e5 2. d4 exd 3. Nf3 Bc5

In general, the Class B player should be content with playing book moves, and the Class A player should be content when his opponent is out of book. Though there is nothing wrong with 3. ..., Bc5, 3. ..., Nc6 is better, transposing into a known Scotch line.

4. Nxd4 Nf6

And now 4. ..., Qf6 5. Be3 Nc6 6. c3 N8e7 is a book line that leaves Black in good shape.

5. Bg5 (23)

White should play 5. Nc3 when Black equalizes with 5. ..., d5! Notice that now Black could play 5. ..., h6 6. Bxf6 (if 6. Bh4 g5 7. Bg3 Nxe4 gains a healthy center

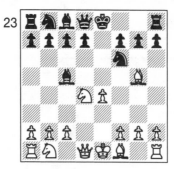

Pawn for free) 6. ..., Qxf6 when Black has gained the two Bishops at no expense in Pawn structure, development, or center influence.

5. ..., d6 6. Bc4 0-0 7. f3

The Class A player solidifies his center Pawn, but the opening hasn't gone too well for him yet. Black seeks further simplification and maintains a good game.

7. ..., Bxd4 8. Qxd4 Nc6 9. Qf2 Be6 10. Bxe6

The Class A player recognizes the dangers of the position. What are they? Black's threatened lead in development, the half-open e-file, his own uncoordinated pieces; thus he willingly simplifies. This is a handy technique to get out of trouble, known to both Class A and Class B players, but notice how successful it is.

10. ..., fxe6 11. Nc3 Qe8 12. 0-0-0 (24)

Though some simplification has occurred, the Class A player would still like to win this game. By castling long, he announces his intention to attack. Can this attack succeed? Analyse the Pawn position. **(25)**

Because White has a majority of Pawns on the kingside of 4 to 3, he has some attacking chances. If Black plays ...,

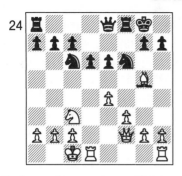

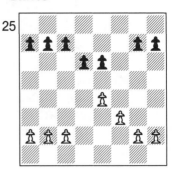

e5, then the square d5 becomes available.White has some minimum chances for the attack to succeed so the Class A player should begin to prepare the Pawn storm to see what happens.

12. ..., a6 13. h4 h6?!

It is the same old story: weakening Pawn moves around the kingfield should be avoided. The Class B player knows this rule, but violates it. Why? he sees White's coming attack. The Bishop seems to be White's most aggressive piece. Drive it back and the attack is lessened. This is not sound logic. The Bishop is mobile. It can flash back and forth across the board. The Pawn on h6 is static, a target. The Class B player does not set up a long range defense, but reacts on a move-to-move basis.

14. Bd2

What is wrong with 14. Be3 ? Analyse.

14. ..., b5 15. Qg3

The move White would like to make here is 15. g4. Is this a sound sacrifice? Don't touch the pieces–analyse 15. g4. If you analysed 15. g4 Nxg4 16. Qg3 N4e5 17. Bxh6 with a plus for White, your tactics are sharp, but you are not taking into account Black's last move. If you analysed 15. g4 b4! 16. Ne2 Nxe4 with a plus for Black, you have the board awareness necessary for a Class A player. The point is that "natural" moves like g4 are highly desirable and should be made unless analysis tells you that something else must be selected. The Class B player is more likely to blunder here and play g4, or defensively, a3. The Class A player makes an aggressive move and is promptly rewarded.

15. ..., Nh5

Is this another example of "reaction" chess? Black drives the Queen away from the attack, but frees the g-Pawn to advance with tempo. This move is only good if Black sees that he can paralyse White's attacking Pawn structure. Can he? Analyse.

16. Qh2 Ne5 17. Rdf1

White labors to get g4 in. Now he would be willing to win two pieces for a Rook after g4, Nxf3; Rxf3 Rxf3; gxh5. Notice that the Class A player is consistent with his plan: attack Black's King by g4. And what of Black's attack?

17. ..., Nc4 18. Be1

This is White's attacking Bishop!

18. ..., b4 19. Ne2 (26)

19. ..., Qc6?!

The Class A player would–or should–find 19. ..., Qa4 20. Kb1 Ne3 21. b3 Qa3 and the threat of Nd1 wins an exchange at least.

20. g4?!

44

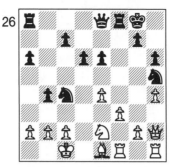

Defense is always the hardest. The theory of a good counter attack holds here...but Black can win material by 20. ..., Ne3 21. Nd4 Nxf1! The Class B player doesn't see it: calculation weakness. The Class A player is right in his choice. Defense is an art the Class A player is not ready to fully master. He is much better off attacking. Masters defend. Class A players attack.

20. ..., Nf6?! 21. Nd4 Qa4 22. Kb1 e5?!

Once again we see the lack of depth in Black's plan: White's Knight is well-placed for defense–drive it away. But Black's attack is almost over. And where will the Knight go?

23. Nf5 Kf7?!

A few moves ago Black was attacking. Now his King is running for cover. An attack must be decisive. The Class A player should go for the jugular.

24. b3 Na3+ 25. Kb2 Qb5 26. g5! (27)

In this fashion–notice how White's attack comes home.

26. ..., hxg6?!

We won't bore the student with proof that White's

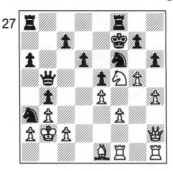

attack is decisive. Let the Class A player verify this for himself. What we would like to show is the difference in defense. Notice how 26. ..., hxg 27. hxg opens up lines for White's Queen, Rook, and Bishop, while 26. ..., Ng8 27. gxh Nxh6 minimizes White's open lines.

27. hxg6 Rh8 28. Qd2!

Analyse White's idea.

28. ..., Nd7 29. g6+!

Shame on you if you selected the Pawn hungry 28. Qxb4. Yes, it would win, but you were attacking furiously two moves ago. Why sell out the attack for a mere Pawn, especially when you can sacrifice one? Remember the jugular?! You need to always be looking for the kill, especially when attacking.

29. ..., Ke6 30. Qg5 Black Resigns

Black resigns–should he? The Class B player should not resign unless he sees specifically how he is going to lose. How is Black going to lose? Analyse a winning combination. Would you resign as Black?

10. DUTCH DEFENSE
White: 1609 player
Black: You

1. d4 e6 2. Nf3 f5

The Dutch Defense can be an effective line against Class B players. Most Class B players are not well booked on the Dutch. This means that they will have to face you on your own territory. When this happens, you will have the advantage because you are the stronger player. Why are you the stronger player? It is a question of will. At this stage of the game (Move 2) you must believe you are the stronger player. There should be no doubt. To believe you will lose is almost always a guarantee that you will lose. Since you are (or shortly will be) a Class A player, you must believe you are stronger than your Class B opponent. Let us see how we can break the will of your opponent.

3. e3 c6

This move announces Black's intention of setting up a Stonewall formation. This attacking formation is defined

47

by the Black Pawn structure d5,c6,e6,f5. Black then usually plays Bd6,Nf6,N8d7,Ne4, Qe8, and Qh5 with attacking chances against White's kingside (further plans might include ..., Rf6 and ..., g5). The flaw in the plan is the weakness at e5. The Dutch is good for a Class A player against a Class B player, but it is probably best avoided against an Expert or stronger.

4. N1d2 d5 5. Be2 Bd6 6. c4 Nd7 (28)

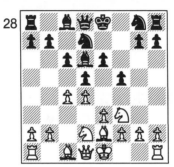

7. c5?!

We have seen this move before (Game 4). Before you check on Game 4, evaluate c5. Why is this move weak? What is Black's plan to take advantage of White's positional error?

7. ..., Bc7

This is the correct retreat, keeping control over e5. This may enable Black to play ..., e5 freeing his game somewhat. After 7. ..., Be7, the Bishop's scope is more limited.

8. b3 N8f6

Black could play 8. ..., e5 9. dxe Nxe5 but after 10. Bb2 White is about equal. Black decides not to relieve the central tension, and to not open up the game when behind in development.

9. Qc2

This is one of those "developing" moves that does nothing. Since e5 is critical and White has already played b3, the proper plan for White was Bb2 (fighting for e5) and, probably after castling, White can try queenside activity by b4, a4, and b5, with chances. On c2 the Queen's influence is dubious.

9. ..., Ne4 10. Bb2 Qf6

Notice the difference in Black's Queen move and White's. Black uses his Queen to pursue positional ideas–control of e5–whereas White's Queen on c2 does nothing to further his game. These ideas are one of the big differences between Class A and Class B. Notice, too, that the Queen is better placed on f6 than e7 as on e7 the influence is only indirect. On f6, too, the Queen supports ..., f4 and there is always the "hidden" threat of ..., Nxc5.

11. h3 (29)

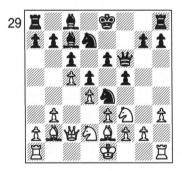

This, too, is typical. The Class B player doesn't know where to place his King. He should have the courage to castle short and defend, but he senses the attack on the kingside. The Class A player knows the King is in just as much danger in the center as on the kingside. The Class A player would then plan to castle short or start queenside operations, but he would not play 11. h3 (General principle: don't move Pawns on the side of the board you are being attacked on).

11. ..., h5 12. Nxe4

Notice White's vacillation. His plan changes from one moment to the next. This is because he has not made a plan to defend his position. This is the kind of chess you as a Class A player must strive to avoid.

12. ..., fxe4

In the Stonewall, Black almost always captures this way to open the f-file and to prepare to free his white-squared Bishop by ..., e5.

13. Nd2 g5 14. Qd1?!

Undeveloping. Can Pawn hunting really be a consideration to a Class A player in this position?

14. ..., 0-0 15. Rf1?!

White passes up his last chance to castle. What is Black's continuation?

15. ..., Nxc5!? (30)

How do you evaluate this move?

16. Bxh5??

White still continues to not understand the position.

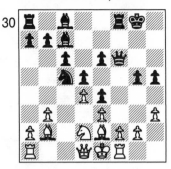

How does Black punish White? Analyse. The Class A player would have found a better way for White to survive. After 16. dxc5!? Qxb2 17. Bxh5 Qg7! Black has the better game, but there is plenty of room to fight.

16. ..., Nd3+ 17. Ke2 Qxf2+ 18. Rxf2 Rxf2 mate

A fitting punishment to the Class B player who leaves his King stuck in the center. If you selected 17. ..., Nxb2 in your analysis on move 15, you are too materialistic. You must learn to "Think King" when attacking. Black showed a solid understanding of the Stonewall formation.

11. ENGLISH OPENING
White: 1685 Player
Black: You

1. c4 e5 2. Nc3 f5

This is a good choice for the Class A player against a Class B player. Why?

3. g3 Nf6 4. Bg2 c6

Black plays to establish a broad Pawn front. This is a good opening to play against a Class B player, who will find it difficult to contain Black's aggression, but not a good choice against a higher-rated opponent.

5. d4 e4 6. f3

This attack on Black's center is reasonable, but Master play prefers 6. Nh3 to post the Knight on f4 (or possibly f2) first.

6. ..., Bb4

Black continues his aggressive play, but 6. ..., d5 is

more logical. Black has prepared his game for ... d5 and should take this opportunity to enforce it. Make necessary moves first. It is not clear whether the Bishop belongs on e7, d6, or b4.

7. Bd2 (31)

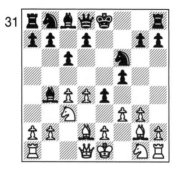

7. ..., d5?

Some errors are inexcusable. If you now selected 7. ..., d5 it is because you are playing without thinking. The Bishop, Knight, Bishop line up on d2,c3,b4 is a trick that all Class A players know–White wins a valuable Pawn by 8. Nxe4! when Black's game is terrible. The opening is not made for automatic moves. The Class A player needs to be careful in selecting his play at any stage of the game.

8. Qb3?

And now you may ask, why does he get away with it? To answer that question we must go into the mind of the Class B player playing a higher-rated opponent. The Class B player does not expect a mistake–he is not looking to punish Black's incorrect play. In other words, he is trusting his opponent to play well. This attitude is a very poor one. The truth of the matter is Class A players make mistakes, that's why they are Class A and not higher. The Class A player *knows* his Class B opponent is going to make errors, and he will play to punish him. As a Class A player, you should always try to be alert to these errors. A healthy skepticism is a desirable attitude for a Class A player.

8. ..., Bxc3

Black kills the guard of e4 and his game is back on track once again.

9. Qxc3 0-0 10. e3

This move does not contribute to White's game. Preferable is 10. Nh3. Where will the Knight go from h3?

10. ..., N8d7 11. c5

Comment on this move. See Games 4 and 10. Would the move be OK if White had his f-Pawn on f4? Analyse. How should Black react to 11. c5 ?

11. ..., exf!?

Black recalls the Nimzovich patent for a wing attack (11. c5): a wing attack is best met by play in the center. As the center is nearly locked, this is Black's best method of opening it up. Black plans to use the e4 square for his pieces. This is an effective plan against White's passive position. Note that if White had his Pawn on f4, this plan wouldn't work. Black would then have to meet the wing attack on the queenside with a wing attack on the kingside, exposing his own King.

12. Nxf3 Ne4 13. Qc2 Qe7 14. Nh4

Once again we see a White King refusing to "castle into it." Yet White must castle or forever keep his Rooks tied up. The Class A player would make definite plans to castle, short or long, in order to get some Rook activity. The Class B player is playing wait-and-see.

14. ..., N7f6 15. Rf1?!

Now White apparently plans to castle long, but at the loss of a critical tempo.

15. ..., Ng4 16. Bxe4

White cannot drive the g4 Knight away by 16. h3 as 16. ..., Nxg3! is strong, and so he must exchange his better Bishop (why is the g2 Bishop "better"?) and open up lines of attack. Black is winning.

16. ..., fxe4 17. 0-0-0 (32)

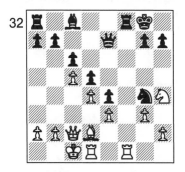

Black to play and win. Analyse without moving the pieces.

17. ..., Nf2! 18. Rde1 Nd3+ 19. Kb1 Nxe1 20. Rxf8+ Qxf8 21. Bxe1 Qf1 (33)

This is a decisive interruption of White's position. White is helpless, but you must plan the conclusion.

22. Qd2 Bg4

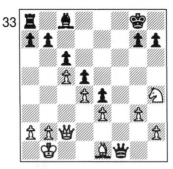

If you planned 22. ..., Bh3! to deprive the Knight of flight squares, you understand this position very well. The text will also win.

23. Ng2 g5! 24. Kc1 Qe2 25. Qxe2 Bxe2 26. a4?

White's last chance, but not much of one, was 26. Bc3 to free e1 for the Knight.

26. ..., Bf3 27. Nf4

White should resign.

27. ..., gxf4 28. gxf Kf7 White Resigns

Except for the error on Move 7, Black played a strong, dynamic game, the kind of play the Class A player should strive for. Key to his win was his understanding that wing play (11. c5) is best met by center play (11. ..., exf!?).

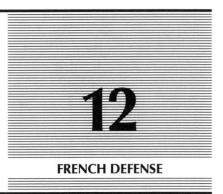
12. FRENCH DEFENSE
White: You
Black; 1625 Player

1. e4 e6 2. d4 d5 3. e5 c5 4. c3 Nc6 5. Nf3 N8e7 6. a3

This move is unnecessary in this variation (development by 6. Bd3 is usual) but it has the value of overprotecting b4, depriving Black of ..., Bb4+ and ..., Nb4 variations.

6. ..., Nf5 7. Bd3 (34)

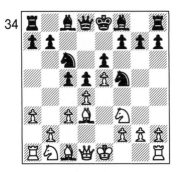

7. ..., Be7

This is another example of the Class B player not thinking in the opening. Since Move 3, Black has been attacking d4. Now he should continue the thematic attack. After all, he has three pieces pressuring d4–his whole position is set up to attack d4–and he plays ..., Be7. Woolly is 7. ..., Qb6 8. Bxf5 exf5 9. cxd Bxc5 10. 0-0 Be6 with a difficult game for both sides. Safer is 7. ..., cxd 8. Bxf5 exf5 9. cxd Be7 and Black is equal. The advanced Pawn can be attacked later by ..., f6 and Black's doubled Pawns will disappear, leaving him with the two Bishops. How does Black foresee all of this? He doesn't have to. He has set his entire position up to play against d4. Given his chance, he passes, not once, but twice.

The Class A player understands the need to continue to logically pursue his goal in the opening (d4 in this game) and would proceed with 7. ..., Qb6 or 7. ..., cxd.

8. 0-0 Bd7?

Again violating the theme: Black mindlessly develops. Analyse how to punish Black. Why can Black be punished? The Class A player knows that Black has twice violated what should be his plan. These violations should leave weaknesses in their wake.

9. Bxf5 exf5 10. dxc5 Be6 11. b4

White has stolen a Pawn and remains with much the better game.

11. ..., Qc7 12. Re1 0-0-0 (35)

Black is just developing–this is not always the best idea. Black's King would be quite safe on the kingside: 12. ..., 0-0 13. Bf4 Rfd8 when White would have a big plus on the queenside, but there would still be a fight. On the

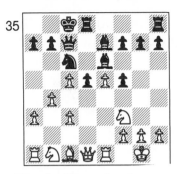

queenside, the Black King is doomed, facing a Pawn avalanche. How does the Class A player know the King is doomed? There are two ways. One, Pawn structure: White has four Pawns to three on the queenside. This means he can eventually pry open Black's King's defenses. On the kingside, the score is four to four–safety. The second method of determining the strength of White's attack is experience. The Class ℬ player who wishes to improve must play chess often. If there is a chess club in your vicinity, make a point to go to it frequently. As a Class A player you will probably be in the upper half of the club. Five minute chess can be a way to improve your game, giving you experience, developing a quicker insight into such positions. Some Masters have said that five-minute chess is bad for your chess game. This may be true of Masters who take their game very seriously, but not being a Master, five minute chess can be very beneficial to you. The important things are to learn from your games and have fun playing. You might record your games for opening study. Don't bother too much with recording the entire game unless it is of tournament time limit.

13. Nd4

A lot can be learned from this move. White doesn't bother "just" developing. He would like to encourage the weakening ..., a6 so that when his b5 comes in, more lines will be opened. The e-Pawn is protected (13. ..., Nxe5? 14.

Bf4 Bf6 15. Qe2 wins) and the possibility of Nb5-Nd6+ is appetizing. Not so good is the more prosaic 13. Bf4 h6! and Black has started a counterattack on White's King.

13. ..., Rd7?!

A move that neither tries to attack (13. ..., g5) nor prevent the Knight from reaching d6 (13. ..., Nxd4 or 13. ..., a6).

14. Nb5 Qb8 15. Nd6+ Kd8 16. Nd2 f6

Black's position is miserable, so we won't fault this opening up of lines near his King. Black's idea is to try to use his superior development–17. exf6 Bxd6 18. cxd6 Qxd6 19. fxg Rxg7, but White chooses to keep his kingside closed.

17. f4 g5 18. Nf3! g4 (36)

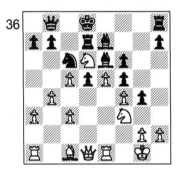

By by-passing f4, even the slim chance of a Black counterattack disappears. White is in full control.

19. Nd4 Nxd4 20. cxd4 h5 21. Bd2

Identify White's plan for placing the Bishop on d2.

21. ..., h4 22. b5 Kc7

After 22. ..., Bxd6 23. exd6, Black will not long survive

either. Prove this to your satisfaction.

23. Ba5+ b6 24. cxb6+ axb6
25. Rc1+ Kd8 26. Bxb6+! Black Resigns

Always be efficient! This is a neat way to end the game.

13. CARO-KANN DEFENSE
White: You
Black: 1645 Player

1. e4 c6 2. c4

Notice how the Class A player immediately puts the Class B player out of his element. The "gentle" Caro-Kann is suddenly a raging central battle. Is this move 2. c4 theoretically "best"? Chess theory is created by Grandmasters: chess struggle is for everyone.

2. ..., e5

Sucess number one–the Caro-Kann has disappeared. The Class B player has been conned out of 2. ..., d5 (the Caro-Kann move). After 3. exd5 Nf6!? Black is in good shape or 3. ..., cxd5 4. cxd5, Black can choose between 4. ..., Nf6 5. Bb5+ Bd7 6. Bc4 or 4. ..., Qxd5 5. Nc3 Qa5 6. d4 Nf6 with healthy play for Black in either case.

3. Nc3

But the Class A player is in strange territory, too. He

should play either 3. d4 (the move ..., c6 took away the center-attacking c6 square from the Knight) or 3. Nf3 d6 4. d4 with good play for White. The Class A aspirant should note this when studying his games so that if this opening should arise again, he will know how to handle it.

3. ..., Bc5 4. f4?! (37)

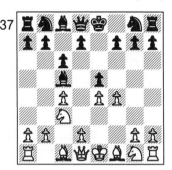

White is inventive in this opening, but inventions in chess don't always turn out well. The weakening of the h4-e1 diagonal can prove embarrassing.

4. ..., Bxg1!?

A well-thought out move. It is no secret that Class B players can reason well on the chess board. Still, chess is a struggle that lasts longer than four moves (usually).

5. Rxg1 exf4

Black has stolen a Pawn and weakened White's kingside. White has a lead in development and space. Which side is better? Let us be kind and say the position is unclear. What should White's immediate plan be?

6. d4

No pussyfooting here! White invites the intensification

of the struggle.

6. ..., Qh4+ 7. g3 fxg3

After 7. ..., Qxh2 8. Rg2! Qh1 9. Bxf4, White is looking very happy and only a Pawn glutton would be happy as Black.

8. hxg Qe7

The opening is over. As a Class A player you should be able to correctly evaluate this position. Do so now. Which side do you prefer? Black has an extra Pawn. White has a strong center and a lead in development. Even chances seems to be a reasonable evaluation. As a Class A player, however, you should prefer White, who has the initiative.

9. Qf3 h6?!

But this move is at least dubious. It neither fights directly to contest the center nor helps Black in development. Black is worried about 9. ..., Nf6 10. Bg5 and so prevents Bg5. This is thinking only for the moment. The Class A player will find 9. ..., d6 10. Be2 Nf6 11. Bg5 N8d7 and later ..., h6 hitting at the bothersome Bishop. This is a plan; 9. ..., h6?! is only a move.

10. Bd3 Nf6 11. Be3 d6 12. g4!?

No automatic moves here. The student can learn from the chess-playing computer in this regard. Even when the move is "obvious," the computer continues to analyse other moves. It evaluates all the moves it is considering before settling on the one it will play. Incidentally, a chess playing program can be of great value to the Class A aspirant. The machine will play you training games whenever you are in the mood. At their upper levels, they are formidable opponents. For around $100 and up, you can find an ideal opponent if there are no humans around of comparable strength. Learn to beat your computer at its upper levels and you will be a Class A player and improving!

Losing would have been 12. 0-0-0? Bg4, but notice how the Class A player is using all his pieces, including the Rook on g1. This is good Class A play.

12. ..., N8d7 13. 0-0-0 Nb6 (38)

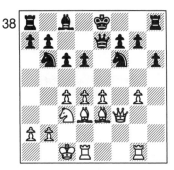

White can no longer develop his pieces. He needs to make specific plans to break into Black's position before Black plays ..., Bd7 and ..., 0-0-0 when the Pawn plus becomes heavier. Obviously White must plan a can opener. Analyse 14. c5, d5, e5, and g5. Which one would you select?

14. e5!?

The Class A player *must* find this move. It is the hallmark of the Class A player who must strive to attack. It is the most desired move on the board, but White has to see the tactical trick–14. ..., dxe5 15. dxe5 Qxe5? 16. Bxb6! winning.

14. ..., Nh7?

The Class B player does not reason as well as the Class A player. The e-file must be kept closed. Therefore 14. ..., dxe5 15. dxe5 Nh7!? 16. Ne4 0-0?! 17. g5! and White's attack is very strong–17. ..., hxg5 18. Nxg5 Nxg5 19. Bxg5 Qc5 20. Rh1 Nxc4 21. Rh8+ and mates. If salvation can be found, and then it takes an Expert or a Master, Black must try 14. ..., dxe5 15. dxe5 Nxg4! 16. Rxg4 Bxg4 17. Qxg4 Qxe5! with strong chances for White after 18. Bd4! The Class B player cannot be faulted for failing to find this line, but he should have found 14. ..., dxe5 first. The reason he doesn't is that he is reacting only to threats and not trying to find a defensive plan for his pieces.

15. exd6

Open e-file, an untouchable d-Pawn, even material, overwhelming lead in development–White should win very quickly.

15. ..., Qf6 16. Qe2

Minus twenty-five rating points for 16. Qxf6. White would win even then but there is bigger game at stake.

16. ..., Be6 (39)

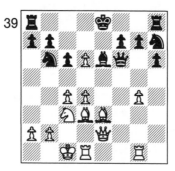

17. d5!

Toujours l'attacque, toujours! White is relentless. What is the (simple) tactical justification for 17. d5 ?

**17. ..., cxd 18. Bxb6 axb6 19.
cxd5 0-0 20. dxe6 fxe6 21. Kb1**

The struggle is over. White keeps his attack and has a big material edge. Resignation is justified at any time now.

21. ..., Ng5 22. Ne4 Black Resigns

14. ENGLISH OPENING
White: You
Black: 1620 Player

1. c4 e5 2. Nc3 f5

A very aggressive choice for the Class B player, and not a bad one–if he has studied the opening. To choose an opening line like this "cold" against a higher rated opponent is usually a subtle form of suicide.

3. e4

The Class A player takes a stand! Also good is 3. g3 and 3. d4!? but the Class A player is willing to take Black's challenge. This is a commendable attitude, not backing away from a fight, and you should adopt it for your own. Be resolute! Attack!

3. ..., d6 4. Nf3 f4?!

We have seen this error from another perspective in earlier games. Correct for Black was 4. ..., Nf6 (Development, center pressure) with about even chances. What is White's correct plan against 4. ..., f4?! Analyse.

5. d4 Nc6 6. d5

While taking central space is not a bad idea, White had better. The use of his superior development (when you have an advantage, try to use it!) might have been capitalized on by 6. dxe!? dxe 7. Qxd8+ Kxd8 8. g3! fxg (not 8. ..., Bg4 9. Ng5 with the advantage) 9. hxg and White has the better game. Why?

6. ..., N6e7 7. b4 (40)

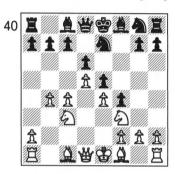

The battle lines are drawn. White plans to exploit his queenside space advantage, and Black plans to operate on the kingside. Notice how the Class A player develops his plan while the Class B player never gets his kingside going. This is a valuable lesson to learn: the better player makes his plan work.

7. ..., Ng6 8. Ba3

The Class A player plans to pressure c5 with all his pieces–Ba3, Rc1, etc. to enforce c5. This plan is all right but requires careful execution.

8. ..., b6 9. Rc1 Nf6 10. Bd3 a5

Black is trying to prevent White's plan–his own chances on the kingside lay far off in a distant future, perhaps even some *other* game. Still, Black is violating the maxim of not moving Pawns on the side of the board one is being attacked on.

11. Rb1

Still keeping the same plan, queenside play, but White had two better plays. Did you choose one of them?–11. 0-0 (King safety) and 11. Qb3 with the idea of 11. ..., axb. Bxb4 when White will follow up with a4 and an eventual a5 to further weaken Black's queenside.

11. ..., axb4 12. Bxb4 Qd7?! (41)

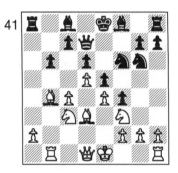

How does this move fit into Black's plan? How does it fit into White's plan? Analyse.

13. c5!

Sharp tactics are a keystone to the Class A player's game. How can the Class B player improve his tactics? There are a number of ways, but two ways are at the top of the list: buy a book on tactics. There are several good books on the market dealing with tactics. They are not only beneficial to the Class A aspirant, they have beautiful ideas that make them a pleasure to read. The second way is to play lots of chess, five-minute, social, or tournament. Those players who are isolated from other chess players, as noted earlier, will find the commercial chess-playing computers especially valuable. The weakness of the computers is mainly positional, but their strong point are tactics. The Class A aspirant can learn much about tactics by playing these machines. One other important option is to play postal chess. This will give you the maximum opportunity to study the position to try to evolve tactics.

13. ...., dxc5?!

Despair? The Class B player gives up much too easily. After 13. ...., Qd8 it is still a fight of sorts. Plan White's continuation after 13. ...., Qd8.

14. Bb5 cxb4 15. Bxd7+ Bxd7 16. Ne2 Rxa2 17. Ra1 (42)

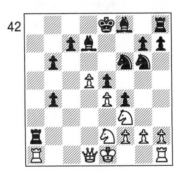

Challenging Black's most active piece. Material is almost even. Black could still plan to make a fight of it if he isn't psychologically depressed. A Class A player with the Black pieces would settle down, count material, and decide that the fight was still on after 17. ...., Rxa1 18. Qxa1 Bd6 19. Qa8+?! Ke7 and there is a lot of play left.

17. ...., b3? 18. 0-0 Bb5?

The careless play of the last few Black moves spotlights his "hopeless" position. Black's position is far from hopeless. What is hopeless is that Black is convinced he is losing to his higher-rated opponent. A losing state of mind has taken over, and a loss is the inevitable result. Black neglects his kingside forces in pursuit of a chimera. The Class A player would not do this.

19. Qxb3

Score one full point on the wall chart.

19. ..., Rxe2? 20. Qxb5+ Black Resigns

The lesson to be learned from this game? The Class A player must resist with all his pieces. He cannot allow the "loss" of a Queen for a near equivalent of material to depress him on the board. At Move 17, the Black forces were down only by a Pawn with plenty of opportunity to fight. The Class B player saw only the negative bank account (Woe is me–I've lost my Queen). Class A players don't have this myopia.

15. ROBATSCH DEFENSE
White: 1624 Player
Black: You

1. e4 Nf6 2. Nc3 d6

The Class A player knows that the 2. .., d5 line leads to equality: 3. e5 d4 4. exf6 dxc3 5. fxg7 cxd2+ 6. Qxd2 Qxd2+ 7. Bxd2 Bxg7= but he chooses to transpose into another opening system he feels will give White more problems.

3. d4 g6 4. f4 Bg7 5. Nf3 0-0 6. Bd3
Nc6 7. 0-0 Bg4 8. Be3 Nd7 (43)

9. Qe1?!

White sees, of course, that a Pawn is going. He apparently believes he will get some play for it. The Class A player knows that to sacrifice a center Pawn, he must get some compensation—a lead in development, greater space, a material advantage, or some positional advantage (weakened kingside). White's "gambit" yields none of these

73

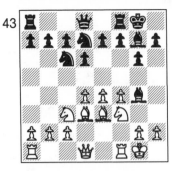

compensations: the Pawn sacrifice is just a Pawn loss. Sounder was 9. e5, or, since Black retreated with 8. ..., Nd7, White can retreat with 9. Ne2. Of the two, since White's game is set up to support e5 (two Pawns covering e5), thematically 9. e5 is the superior play.

9. ..., Bxf3 10. Rxf3 Nxd4 11. Bxd4?!

Since White sacrificed the Pawn for a nebulous attack, he should not be swapping wood: 11. Rh3, to keep as many pieces on the board, is better.

11. ..., Bxd4+ 12. Kh1 Bg7

Black has a "won" game, but the technique for winning this position is not necessarily within the ability of a Class A player nor expert. Gary Kasparov or Anatoly Karpov playing the White pieces should still always be able to beat the Class A player. What then is the meaning of technique for the Class A player? Here it should mean that if Black plays solidly, he should defeat his lesser-rated opponent. But isn't that true on Move one? The Class A player should not rely on "won" games winning themselves. It is not enough to have a good game; one must continue to play well. We will carefully watch the Class A player's "technique."

13. Rh3 e6 14. Qg3 Nc5

74

Black's last two moves were good–..., e6 kept the enemy Queen away from his King and ..., Nc5 will allow Black to swap off the potentially attacking Bishop.

15. Re1 c6

Where is Black's extra Pawn? It is the Pawn on d6. The Class A player knows he must use his extra Pawn and so, properly, prepares its advance. In this way he makes the extra Pawn do some work. Otherwise it just sits back and does not make its "extraness" count.

16. f5

White, on the other hand, must attack even though his attack should not succeed. Why should his attack not succeed? Because he can attack only with Queen, Rook, Pawn, and maybe Knight and Rook. Black can defend with Queen, Rook, Bishop, and his King and Pawns.

16. ..., exf5 17. exf5 Nxd3 18. Qxd3 d5 (44)

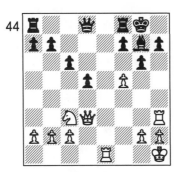

Black advances his extra Pawn, taking away center squares from the enemy Knight.

19. Nd1 Re8

Both sides know that all exchanges favor Black. Thus

White is pushed away from the only open file.

20. Rf1 Qd6 21. Qf3 Re7!

Patient defense. Notice the Class A player does not automatically reject 21. ..., Re7 because 22. f6 will "win a piece." He looks a little deeper and finds a move that guards f7 and prepares to double on the open e-file.

22. Ne3 d4

This is strong play. Notice, however, that Black could continue 22. ..., R8e8 as 23. Ng4 Re1 24. f6 could be met by 24. ..., Rxf1+ 25. Qxf1 Bxf6! 26. Nxf6+ Qxf6.

23. fxg6 fxg6 24. Ng4 h5!

Black can calculate that this weakening will not harm his game and so may correctly violate that general principle.

25. Nf6+?

A blunder in the face of Black's sound defensive strategy, but even after 25. Nf2 Rf8 26. Qd1 R7f7 Black has a strong, winning game, and White's attack has disappeared.

25. ..., Bxf6 26. Rg3

Too late White sees 26. Qxf6 Qxf6 27. Rxf6 Re1+ mates next.

26. ..., Bg7 27. Qb3+ Kh7 White Resigns

This may have seemed like an effortless win on the part of the Class A player, a walkover. Actually there is much here for the Class A aspirant to learn from. Black's solid play, relentless and strong, is the mark of a Class A player on his way to Expert. The Class A player who can play this clearly might benefit from *How To Become a Candidate Master* by (shameless plug!) Alex Dunne. But seriously, this is Class A playing at its best. The Class B opponent never had a chance. This is how you should strive to play.

16. MORRA GAMBIT
White: You
Black: 1759 Player

1. e4 c5 2. d4 cxd4 3. c3 dxc3 4. Nxc3 Nc6 5. Nf3 e5

This is a very committing move for the Black player to make: the square d5 falls into White's control, the diagonal a2-g8 belongs to White, and Black's extra Pawn, the one on d7, remains severely backward. Black would do better to adopt a defensive posture by 5. ..., e6, ..., d6, ..., Nf6, ..., Be7, and ..., 0-0, etc.

The Morra is very difficult to play as Black. Patient defense is not the Class B player's strong point. For this reason, we suggest 3. ..., Nf6 as a safer way of declining the gambit.

6. Bc4 h6?! (45)

The Class B player knows this move violates general principles, but he finds that f7 has become a sensitive square. He sees that 6. ..., Nf6 is met by 7. Ng5 and rejects

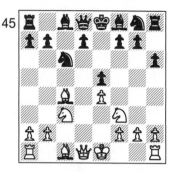

that line. Black's best is not to hold on to the gambit Pawn, but prepare to give it back. Class A players know this idea and *use it!* A Class A player opponent might try 6. ..., Nf6 and the game might continue 7. Qb3 d5! 8. Nxd5 Nxd5 9. Bxd5 Bb4+ 10. Kf1 Qe7 or 7. Ng5 d5! 8. Nxd5 Nxd5 9. Bxd5 Bb4+ 10. Kf1 [10. Bd2 Qxg5 11. Bxc6+ bxc6 12. Bxb4 Qxg2 13. Qd6!? Qxe4+! and Black is better] Be6! and Black is OK. White, of course, can avoid these lines by 7. 0-0. The point is that the Class A player seeks active, forward going development of his pieces. The Class B player finds his "solution" by one-goal plans that often do not further his game.

The study of Master games will illustrate this principle, and going over these games will greatly benefit the Class B player. He may not grasp all that the Master game can offer, but he can learn pieces along the way to apply in his own games. He should try to apply these principles. Moves like 6. ..., h6?! should be anathema to him. A philosophy to follow is that if you have to play moves like this in the opening, find a new opening.

7. 0-0 Nf6 8. Qe2 Be7 9. Rd1 a6 10. Be3 Ng4

Here, too, is a typical Class B error. Black has been setting up a solid defensive position. Now he strikes out in a brief flurry of activity. His few developed pieces challenge an army that is almost fully mobilized. Such tactics will fail against the Class A player. A better plan was complete mobilization by ..., d6, ..., Be6, ..., 0-0, etc.

11. Bd2 Bc5?! (46)

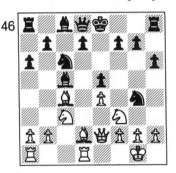

Black's Bishop and Knight are taking on too great a task. You as a Class A player should know how to punish Black. What is your plan?

12. Bxf7+! Kf8

Black should have taken, if just to eliminate one attacker.

13. Be1 Bxf2+?!

Pigheadedness! Black insists on challenging the superiorly developed White, playing with his queenside forces out of commission. The Class A player has got to be content. Why is Black doing this? The lure of materialism is hard to resist.

14. Bxf2 Nxf2?

After 14. ..., Kxf7 15. Qc4+ Black cannot be happy, but the fight would go on after 15. ..., Kg6. Why can't the Class B player find this line? Some will, some won't. Those who don't, don't calculate but play the game move by move.

15. Qxf2 Qf6

Now the Class B player calculates 15. ..., Kxf7 and discovers 16. Ng5+ leads to mate. Should he be surprised?

16. Bb3 (47)

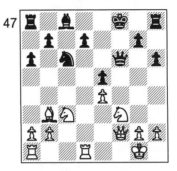

White has the attack and an extra piece. You should plan to win quickly. What happens next is not pretty. Not all chess games can be beautiful, but they can be efficient. It is the Class A player's job to be efficient and dispatch his opponent as painlessly as possible.

16. ..., Ke8 17. Nd5 Qd8 18. Qg3 g5 19. Nxe5 Rb8

Everything loses.

20. Nxc6 bxc6 21. Qe5+! Black Resigns

Subtract a point for the over-greedy 21. Qxb8. What has this silly Rook to do with the game? Mate is much more important.

17. STONEWALL DEFENSE
White: You
Black: 1605 Player

1. f4

The Bird's Opening is often used by Class A players because of its clear-cut strategic plan: control of e5, occupation of e5 by a Knight, recapture (possibly) with the f-Pawn with chances for a kingside attack based on the half-open f-file and the strong Pawn on e5. But why play an opening that the Masters don't play? The Class A player needs to learn to think for himself in the opening. To play by rote, to duplicate Master openings simply because the openings are popular, is not learning to think. Masters should play Master openings. Class A players should play chess. As you get stronger, you will play stronger openings.

1. ..., d5 2. Nf3 Nf6 3. e3 g6 4. c3 Bg7 5. d4 (48)

White has now set up a Stonewall Formation–a reverse Dutch, if you will. White's plan is still about the same as mentioned above. As an exercise, turn the board around.

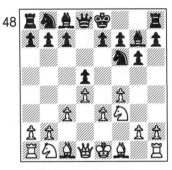

What should Black's plan be? Notice that two of his pieces, the Bishop on g7 and the Pawn on d5 are committed. How is Black to handle the center? By analysing what you think Black's best plan should be, you can plan to take advantage of moves that do not fit into this plan.

The Class A player playing Black would eye the e4 square hungrily and play to occupy it with his pieces. Possible is 5. ..., Bf5 (e4!) 6. Qb3 Qc8 7. Be2 0-0 8. 0-0 N8d7 9. N1d2 c5 10. h3 h5 11. Nh4 c4! 12. Qd1 Be4 13. Nxe4 Nxe4 14. Qe1 b5 with good play for Black.

5. ..., 0-0 6. Bd3 N8d7 7. N1d2 c5 8. 0-0 b6 9. b4

An interesting sideline: White wishes to clarify the battle on d4. We have often seen Class B players play ..., c4 in analogous positions. A quiz: why would 9. ..., c4 be weak here and yet recommended on Move 11 of the above paragraph? Examine the two positions. What is your conclusion?

The answer is that White would benefit from ..., c4 as he has excellent chances of conquering e4. When ..., c4 takes pressure off the center, e4 opens it up with a favorable position. In the above example (the note to 5. ..., Bf5), White has little chance of conquering e4 as this square belongs to Black.

9. ..., cxb4

83

Prematurely releasing the tension. The Class A player would see that White cannot advantageously exchange twice on c5 so he would complete his minor piece development with 9. ..., Bb7. This might enable him to capture the c-file by a properly timed ..., Rc8. Then he could try ..., cxb with chances to gain an advantage.

10. cxb4 Qc7?! (49)

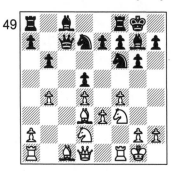

Black is not thinking clearly. White will play what? Analyse White's best plan.

11. Bb2

Of course. White will soon play Rc1 and gain the c-file with tempo. Such plays are stock techniques of the Class A player. But how does the c-file influence White's concern with the center? Watch how White is *thinking* rather than just moving plastic.

11. ..., Bb7 12. a4

White occupies a little more queenside space. This is just a prelude to his real plan.

12. ..., a6

Typical–Black is playing reaction chess, dancing to

White's tune. A Class A player playing Black would look for a more active defense.

13. Qb1!?

This is an interesting idea worthy of study. What is the idea behind Qb1!? Do you approve? Notice that when White takes control of e4, Black's source of counterplay by ..., Ne4 disappears leaving White with a significant edge. This is solid, smart Class A play. By vacating the d1-square, White prepares to bring his King Rook to the c-file with strong pressure on the queenside. This illustrates the difference between thinking and moving. As a Class A player you should try to think like this: solve the problem of the center squares and piece activity.

13. ..., e6?!

Aimless Black play–the weakness of the Class B player. He has not prepared a plan of defense. The Class A player knows Black should seek exchanges and would continue with 13. ..., Rac8 14. Rc1 Qb8 and exchanges will soon occur on the c-file. In the battle between thought and nought, thought will win.

14. Rc1 Qb8 15. Ne5

At last the Knight appears on e5. Black's idea of swapping it off is suspect because of his passive game. Black should now play 15. ..., Rc8.

15. ..., Nxe5?! 16. dxe5 Ng4?! (50)

Black has but one active piece–his Knight on g4. This false activity, too, is a sign of the Class B player. Such single active pieces are doomed to failure. Why? Let us watch how the Class A player now takes advantage of Black's

85

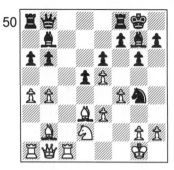

disorganized position.

17. Bd4!

Combining attack, defense, and centralization all in one play. Centralized pieces are stronger workers than pieces shunted off to the side.

17. ..., Qd8

Black, too, tries combining attack and defense, but White's position is too strong now. This strength has been gained by White's thoughtful play. There are no accidents in chess.

18. Nf3

Forethought! This play is much better than 18. h3 Nh6. From f3 the Knight prevents the incursion of the Black Queen and, more important, the Knight will find an ideal square on d4 after the Bishop moves.

18. ..., f5?!

Such "active" moves from a fundamentally defensive position should be avoided, but the player below Master finds them hard to resist. The weakening of the e-Pawn will prove fatal.

19. a5 b5 20. Bb6 Qb8 21. h3 Nh6 22. Nd4 (51)

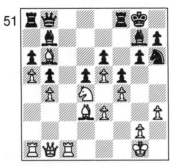

White's minor pieces are ideally posted–Black's position is ripe to fall apart.

22. ..., Re8 23. Rc7 Bf8 24. Ra3 Bc8?

In difficult positions, blunders are easy to find because there are so many of them. The Class A player should be able to plan a win after 24. ..., Nf7. Try it. Do not move the pieces–give White's general winning line. After 25. Rac3 Nd8 (If 25. ..., Nh6 26. Rxb7! Qxb7 27. Rc7 Qb8 28. Nc6 wins) 26. Rd7 and Black is helpless. Analyse and prove this to yourself.

25. Nc6 Black Resigns

18. FRENCH DEFENSE
White: 1620 Player
Black: You

1. e4 e6 2. d4 d5 3. Nc3 Bb4 4. Bd2

Although this has been played by Alekhine, it is good for equality at best–against a Grandmaster. Stronger is the standard 4. e5, gaining space–if Black knows how to handle 4. Bd2.

Now you, as a Class A player, have to decide Black's next move. What do you play?

4. ..., Bxc3

If you selected this exchange, then the Class B player's gamble to take you out of the book has succeeded. Correct was 4. ..., dxe4 5. Qg4 (Not 5. Nxe4 Qxd4! with the advantage) 5. ..., Nf6 6. Qxg7 Rg8 and Black is in good shape.

This brings up an important point: is it worth while for the aspiring Class A player to study annotated Master games? The answer is yes for at least two important reasons. First, the study of Master games may well include this specific position. The Class A player is more familiar with the term "book," but that is what "book" is–how Masters handled this particular position. It is especially helpful when the Masters explain the thought behind their choice of moves rather than just give the move played in the game. The second reason it helps to study annotated games is that a good writer can help the Class A player to learn to think in chess terms to select a move. Here the Master may well explain that the extra center Pawn, accelerated development, and the looseness of White's d-Pawn give Black an easy game to play. This gives the Class A player an insight into how to handle analogous positions. By reading Master games, the Class A player can learn how to hone his thinking. Not all of it will "take," but each step forward increases your understanding of the game.

5. Bxc3 dxe4 6. d5 (52)

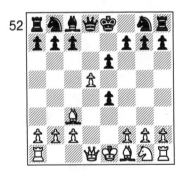

Comment on this move. Notice that White, though a Pawn down, has a lead in development and definite threat. Notice, too, that 6. Qg4 Nf6 7. Qxg7 Rg8 8. Qh6 gives White fair play as his d-Pawn is secure (consult the above paragraph). What should Black play?

6. ..., Nf6

Of course! Now White's Pawn advance has been identified as premature–he will have to advance Black's game when the e-Pawn will be secure. What can be learned from this (slightly) misplayed opening? If you choose to play an off-beat line (4. Bd2) you should be familiar with the strategic ideas of the opening and not just play something to get your opponent out of book.

The Class B player often does not assess his advantages and disadvantages–he is just "playing chess."

7. Bb5+ Bd7 8. Bxd7+ Qxd7 9. dxe6 Qxe6 10. Bb4 (53)

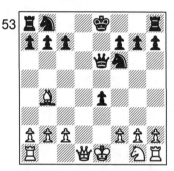

White prevents Black from castling, but someone should have reminded him about developing his pieces. Black's lead in development could become painful. As a prospective Class A player, what continuation would you try here?

10. ..., N8d7

If you selected this passive line in order to play ..., c5 to drive the White Bishop back and castle kingside, subtract ten rating points. If you selected it to castle queenside and use your superior space and development, you have Class A opening strength. If you selected the very aggressive 10. ..., Nc6 11. Ba3 Rd8 12. Qe2 Nd4, go to the head of the class–you will be a Class A player in no time.

11. Qd4

White insists on preventing you from castling on either wing. How do you proceed now? Analyse the position- but come up with an *idea,* not just a move. Remember you have an opponent across the board from you who wants to beat you.

11. ..., Ne5!

Good! The Class A way: aggressive piece play to gain your objective. The threat of ..., Nc6 gains more time. Note how the Class A player rejects such non-forwarding moves as ..., a5 or ..., b6, though a favorable word could be said for ..., b6.

12. Qc5 0-0-0!

The Class A player knows the advantage of develop- ment. The a-Pawn is intrinsically meaningless. By castling, he keeps White's King in the center facing almost all of Black's pieces. White is in big trouble.

13. Qxa7

How do you continue after 13. Ne2? If you found 13. ..., Nd3+ 14. cxd3 exd3 15. Qe3 Qxe3 16. fxe3 dxe2 with an advantage, you understand what is going on.

13. ..., Nf3+ 14. gxf3 exf3+ 15. Qe3 Qc4 16. Be7

If you did not see this White resource, set the pieces back up before your 13th move. Analyse again. See, in your mind's eye, the continuation 16. Be7. What can you do now?

16. ..., Nd5 17. Qa7 (54)

17. ..., Qe4+!

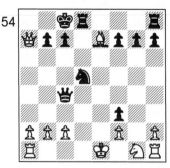

The Class A player does not mechanically recapture: he is too strong for that. He follows Tarrasch's dictum–"If you see a strong move, sit on your hands." There may be a stronger move on the board.

18. Kf1

What is the checkmate in two after 18. Kd1 ?

18. ..., Qc4+ 19. Ke1 Rhe8

Black wins with this move, but stronger is 19. ..., Rde8. It is academic, however.

20. Qa8+ Kd7 21. Qxd8+ Rxd8 22. Bxd8 Kxd8 23. c3

Though material is roughly even (Queen and Pawn vs. two Rooks) the position is not. White's Knight cannot move–23. Nxf3 Qe4+ wins or 23. Nh3 Qe2 mate. If the Knight cannot move, White's King Rook is immobile, and White can only fight with his Rook against Queen and Knight–terribly unfair odds. The Class A player knows he has his opponent hooked.

23. ..., Nf4

Stronger than 23. ..., Nxc3 which would also win.

24. Rd1+ Nd3+ 25. Kd2

Nxf2 26. Nxf3 Nxh1 White Resigns

After 27. Rxh1 the ending is hopeless for White. How would you win this as Black? If you answered the advance of the f-Pawn and making a new Queen, you understand the ending. You should. It is simple enough. A plebeian way of beginning, but as good as most, is 27. ..., Qxa2.

19. RUY LOPEZ
White: 1676 Player
Black: You

1. e4 e5 2. Nf3 Nc6 3. Bb5 a6 4. Bxc6

This is a good line for the lower-rated player to play against you, the Class A player. That is because the handling of the two Bishops is a technique of Masters and strong Experts. Since Black's compensation in the Exchange Variation of the Ruy Lopez is the two Bishops, the Exchange Variation may mean trouble for you.

4. ..., dxc6 5. 0-0 Bg4

Though the Masters prefer 5. ..., f6 to encourage White to open up the center for Black's Bishops, this line is also not a bad choice. The implication of 5. ..., Bg4, however, is that Black will eventually play ..., Bxf3 and the two Bishops will go.

94

6. h3 h5

Playing 6. ..., Bxf3 immediately is too much of a pantywaist choice. The Class A player must strive to make the opening difficult for his opponent and 6. ..., h5 has that idea in mind. For White to capture the Bishop–7. hxg4 hxg4 8. Nxe5 Qh4 9. f3 g3–is immediately fatal.

7. d3 Bxf3?!

The Class A player who is unfamiliar with this opening should analyse 7. .., Qf6. Do it now! Is it playable? Analyse. Don't touch the pieces, do it in your head. If you saw 7. ..., Qf6 8. hxg4 hxg4 9. Ng5 Qh6 10. Nh3 your calculating ability is on Class A level. If you then saw 10. ..., Qh5! with the better chances, you have very strong powers of analysis. For the Class A player 7. ..., Qf6! is a power of knowledge rather than calculation. A well-prepared Class A player can be a powerful force. Note: After 7. ..., Qf6 8. N1d2, White still has a minimal edge.

8. Qxf3 Be7 9. Nc3 Qd7 (55)

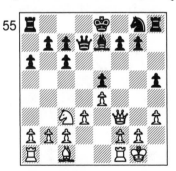

The weakness of Black's game is the fact he has little scope for active play. There are no good plans for queenside activity because of his doubled Pawns. The loosening effect of ..., h5 does not offer much scope on the kingside. The center belongs to White. The advantage belongs to your opponent. Your job is to hold him at bay, avoid further weaknesses, and eventually take the initiative away from him. This is a difficult task. You have a hard game ahead of you. The Class A player should dig in with a "tough" mental attitude.

10. Ne2

Repositioning the Knight toward more productive squares.

10. ..., Nf6 11. Ng3 g6 12. Bg5 Nh7 13. Bxe7 Qxe7

In whose favor was the exchange of Bishops? The Class A player should be able to tell it favors him–his Bishop was defensive and slightly bad (Pawns on the same color squares); White's was aggressive and good. The exchange makes life a little easier for him, but any thoughts of winning must be a long way off.

14. Qe3 h4 15. Ne2 g5

Preventing the desirable f4, Black keeps White's game in check.

16. d4 (56)

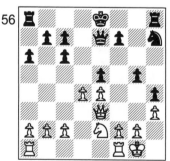

Correctly, White opts to open up the center. Black is

now faced with some unpleasant choices–16. ..., 0-0-0?!
17. dxe5 Qxe5 18. Qa7! and Black's game is disrupted.
Equally unpleasant is 16. ..., 0-0 17. dxe5 Qxe5 18. f4! and
White has a powerful attack. What is Black to do? Class A
players should be resourceful.

16. ..., Nf6!?

This is the resourcefulness of which we spoke. White's
e-Pawn can prove to be weak, too. Throwing the game into
a tactical fight with open lines against White's King must
be an appetizing choice to the Class A player and he
should strive to find such choices.

17. Qxg5 Rh5!

This is the resource you had to find. This aggressive
attitude will pay off in many extra points on the wall charts.

18. Qe3 0-0-0!

Another nice play on the part of the Class A player.
Now 19. dxe5 Qxe5 20. Qa7 Nxe4! as 21. Qa8+ Kd7 22.
Rad1 + Nd6 is winning for Black.

19. Rad1 exd4 20. Nxd4 Qxe4
21. Qxe4 Nxe4 22. Nf3 (57)

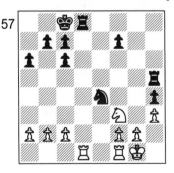

97

Black still has his doubled queenside Pawns, but he has active pieces and White's kingside Pawn majority has been held in check. His adventuresome play beginning with 15. ..., g5 has paid off, a small dividend, but such are the beginnings of great fortunes. Now no Class A player would exchange Rooks. Why?

22. ..., Rg8 23. Rd4 Ng5 24. Rg4!? f5

Not bad was 24. ..., Nxf3+ ruining White's Pawn structure, but White keeps his chances as his Rooks become very active. The text eliminates White's two active pieces and prepares a King advance on the queenside, if necessary.

25. Rxg5 Rhxg5 26. Nxg5 Rxg5 27. Kh2 f4 28. Rg1

White is now fully ready for g3 but Black has found new ground for his Rook. The truth of the matter is the Class A player knows that piece activity is as important in the ending as the middle game. That has been Black's theme throughout this game, and now it begins to pay handsomely.

28. ..., Re5! (58)

29. g3

Having said A ...

29. ..., Re2

Of course! This invasion is now devastating.

30. Rg2?!

White continues to show he does not know what Class A players know–Rooks must be active. After 30. gxh4!? White stays in the fight, and after 30. ..., Rxc2 31. h5 Rc5 32. Rg4 Rxh5 33. Rxf4 the game is even–White has activated his Rook.

**30. ..., f3 31. Rg1 Rxf2+ 32. Kh1 hxg3
33. Rxg3 Rxc2 34. Rxf3 Rxb2 35. h4 Rxa2
36. h5 Ra5 37. Rh3 Rg5 White Resigns**

Black gets back in time to win– 38. h6 Rg8 39. h7 Rh8 etc.

20. TWO KNIGHTS' DEFENSE
White: 1700 Player
Black: You

1. e4 e5 2. Nf3 Nf6 3. Bc4

This is the Boden-Kieseritzky Gambit, and it is very dangerous for Black to accept if he is unfamiliar with it. The unbooked Class A player is advised to steer the game into more familiar channels. The Class A aspirant who likes to can explore some of the older opening books–ca. 1890. There are usually some exciting attacking lines that haven't been seen for ninety years. These attacking lines may fail against Masters, but they can add spice and points to your tournament games. They will also teach you much about the open game, a necessity for the Class A player to know.

3. ..., Nc6 4. Ng5 d5 5. exd5 Nxd5 6. Nxf7!? (59)

This is the famous Fegatello or Fried Liver Attack. It is

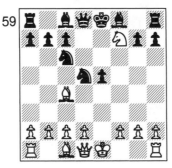

a dangerous line, and the player of the Black forces should not allow it. The Fegatello does not lead to a forced win, nor even necessarily the better game for White. Why then not allow it? Isn't an extra piece an extra piece? The Class A player's defensive skills as Black in this position are usually not superior to the Class B's attacking skills, and with his King stationed in the middle of the board, many bad things can happen.

6. ..., Kxf7 7. Qf3+ Ke6

Retreating just loses a valuable Pawn with a ruined game.

8. Nc3 Nb4

White gets the better chances after 8. ..., Ne7 9. d4 c6 10. Bg5 h6 11. Bxe7 Bxe7 12. 0-0-0 Rf8 13. Qe4 Bg5+ 14. Kb1 Rf4 15. Qxe5+ Kf7 16. Nxd5 cxd5 17. Bxd5+ Kf8 18. Bb3. Analyse 13. ..., Rxf2 to a Black loss (known since the 1600s!).

9. Qe4

Also playable and very complicated is 9. a3. The text is more positional. The player looking for a quick win might try 9. a3 though–how should Black procede after 9. a3 Nxc2+ 10. Kd1 ? Minus rating points if you selected 10. ...,

Nxa1 which fits into White's plan after 11. Nxd5 Kd7 12. d4! with a strong attack. You were a Knight ahead with a King in the middle of the board. So why take a defensive piece (N on b4), exile it to a1 and unleash White's attack–all for a miserable Rook that isn't even in the game? Plus points for 10. ..., Nd4! with complicated play. The Class A player cannot let material considerations outweigh King safety.

9. ..., c6 10. a3 Na6 11. d4 Nc7 (60)

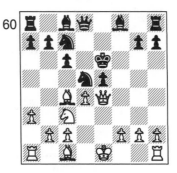

12. O-O

This natural move is too slow–White could try either 12. f4 or 12. Bf4 (open lines or development). Notice that 12. Qxe5+ Kf7 just drives the Black King into safety. Now you have a problem. What plan can you evolve for King safety? Once White's Rooks reach e1 and d1 the Black King will self-destruct if he remains in the center.

12. ..., Qd6!

Not so much to guard the e-Pawn but to find a hiding place for the King. The Class A player plans his defense, not just falls into it.

13. Bf4 Kd7! 14. dxe5 Qg6!

The Class A player knows that the exchange of pieces

lessens White's attacking chances. By judicious offers to exchange Queens he slows up White's attack until it is nonexistant and the extra piece tells. You should be able to analyse that 15. Qxg6 hxg6 16. e6+ Ke8! is insufficient for White.

15. Bxd5

White wishes to avoid 15. Qd4 Ne6, but this means another piece comes off and Black's defensive chores are lessened. Notice what is happening here is very important: the Class A player came up with a *plan* of defense starting with 12. ....., Qd6! By sticking to this plan, Black is outplaying his opponent who only *wants* to attack.

15. ...., cxd5 16. Qd4 Qc6! 17. Rad1 Bc5 18. Qd3 d4 (61)

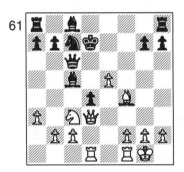

Black's excellent defensive play is the sign of a strong Class A player and much can be learned by replaying moves 12-18. Black has only to solve the problem of his Queen Bishop and King before going over to the initiative with his extra piece. How can this be done? Think.

19. Ne4 Ne6 20. Nxc5+

Every exchange favors Black. Why? Better was 20. Bg3 with some hopes based on f4 and f5, but the Class B player may be becoming discouraged here.

20. ..., Qxc5 21. Bg3 b5 22. c3 Bb7 23. Qf5 (62)

Class A players can benefit from Aron Nimzovich's *My System* which discusses the theory of the blockade. After 23. cxd4 Qd5 24. f3 Rac8, White's Pawns are securely blockaded and Black has a strong initiative brewing. To avoid this paralysis, White goes on a fishing expedition. Best was 23. cxd4, anyway. Why?

23. ..., Raf8!

Always forceful!–the Class A player knows well the value of the initiative. Watch how his active pieces quickly overcome White's "attack."

24. Qg4 h5! 25. Qh3 g5! (63)

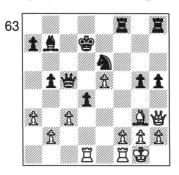

Black has all the play–White's attack has been reduced to an active Rook against all of Black's working pieces. The game is almost over.

26. Rxd4+ Ke7 27. Rd6 Bc8 28. Kh1

White could also resign. Black's fine defensive play has paid off handsomely.

28. ..., Nf4 29. Bxf4 Bxh3 30. Bxg5+ Kf7 31. f4

White should resign. Hopeless, too, is 31. gxh3 Qxe5 32. Rd7+ Ke8 33. Re7+ Qxe7.

31. ..., Bg4 32. f5 Qxe5 33. Rf6+ Qxf6!

The simplest, after which there is no resistance.

**34. Bxf6 Kxf6 35. h3 Be2 36. Rf2 Bc4
37. Rf4 Re8 White Resigns**

If you are ever defeated in such a decisive fashion, control your emotions. Ask your opponent for a postmortem. Learn from your opponent's ideas. There is no sin in being outplayed. Not wanting to know how you were outplayed, however, is one sure way of never advancing.

21. PETROFF'S DEFENSE
White: You
Black: 1683 Player

1. e4 e5 2. Nf3 Nf6

The Petroff has had the reputation as a drawish open-ing for a number of years. This reputation is not fully deserved, but as White you have to show your Class B oppo-nent you are not interested in an early draw.

3. Nxe5 d6

Every Class A player must know how to win against 3. ..., Nxe4. If you don't, find out. Either analyse the position on your own, or go to an opening book. Knowledge is power.

4. Nf3 Nxe4 5. d4

Why doesn't White usually chase the Knight away

with 5. d3 Nf6 6. d4 d5 with the advantage of the first move in a symmetrical position? The reason is White intends to prove the Knight is prematurely posted on e4 and will have to retreat, costing Black another tempo.

5. ..., d5 6. Bd3 Nc6 7. c3 (64)

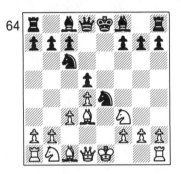

But this is not following White's plan–the d-Pawn can be further attacked by c4, weakening the base of the Knight on e4. Better, then, was 7. 0-0 and White will play c4 when Black has problems.

7. ..., Bf5 8. 0-0 Bd6 9. Re1 Qf6 10. N1d2 Qg6

Black has expanded his forces to maintain the Knight on e4, but he has lost time and his King is stuck in the center. Plan to take advantage of these factors.

11. Nxe4?!

You probably found 11. Nh4 Qf6 12. Nxf5 Qxf5 13. f3 winning a piece outright–13. ..., Qh5 14. Nf1. Why did our Class A player miss this? Answer: he missed it because he saw a strong line to give him an advantage. "When you see a strong move, sit on your hands!"–Tarrasch. The Class A player looked a little deeper into the position, but he is wrong nevertheless. This method is safe, and strong, but 11. Nh4 is decisive. Simple chess is frequently the best, but

Class A players thrive on tactics. White should have found 11. Nh4. What's Black's best move now?

11. ..., dxe4? (65)

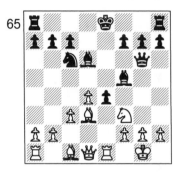

This is the blunder that answers White's error. After 11. ..., Bxe4! (control of e4?!) White only wins a Pawn– 12. Ng5 0-0 but White still has a sizeable advantage. The Class B player is being coaxed into making bad moves. This happens frequently because Class B players frequently believe their opponents. A Class A player, bound to resist, would have found 11. ..., Bxe4.

12. Nh4 Qf6 13. Nxf5 0-0-0

The Knight is taboo–13. ..., Qxf5 14. Bxe4 wins at least a piece for White. This is what the Class A player foresaw on move 11.

14. Nxd6+ cxd6 15. Bxe4 d5 16. Qg4+

Comment on this move.

16. ..., Kb8 17. Bd3

If you thought 17. Qf4+ Qxf4 18. Bxf4+ Ka8 19. Bd3 (or 19. Bf3) was a better plan, you are right. This was a better plan, swapping Queens to achieve an easily won ending. You are thinking like a Class A player.

17. ..., Rde8 18. Bf4+ Ka8 19. Bg3 h5 20. Qd7

Come on, now. If you liked this move, you need to review your tactics. Comment on 20. Qxh5.

20. ..., Rd8 21. Qf5

Observe how ineffecient White's play has been. He could have exchanged Queens on Move 17–which you decided was the right plan. Instead he has played rather aimlessly until now, five moves later, he comes back to the Queen exchange. He has broken the rule of Class A play: *Thou shalt not shilly-shally.* The extra piece has prevented Black from doing anything, but you will not always have such luxuries as an extra piece.

21. ..., Qxf5 22. Bxf5 g6 23. Bd3 h4 24. Be5 Rh5

You still have to win this game. What is your plan?

25. Re3 Rg8 26. Rael g5 27. Bd6

This is the right plan: Simplify and attack.

27. ..., a6 28. Bc5 g4

Black could resist–but why should he–by 28. ..., R5h8.

29. Re8+ Rxe8 30. Rxe8+ Nb8 31. Bd6 Ka7

Black should really resign, but since he won't, put him away. Analyse!

32. Bxb8+ Kb6 33. b4 Rg5 34. Rd8 Black Resigns

This was not a pretty game. Sometimes chess has to

be cruel. There are lessons to be learned. White's play was uneven. Why? Because he wanted to attack when the position called for simplification. It is the position on the board that should determine your plans, not your desires.

22. SICILIAN DEFENSE
White: 1635 Player
Black: You

1. e4 c5

The "choice" between 1. ..., e5 and all the rest of the Black defenses is very personal. With a move such as 1. ..., c5, Black plans to "outwit" his opponent, to outplay him in positional or tactical situations because of their complexity. This is one of the true ways of chess and should always be respected.

2. Nf3 d6 3. d4 cxd 4. Nxd4 Nf6 5. Nc3 a6

For students (as opposed to practical players) a book on the history of the Najdorf Variation can be very valuable. Such a book allows the student to view the historical development of the defense and its ideas.

6. f4

This is the Levenfish Variation, not without merit but not as popular as 6. Bg5, 6. Bc4, 6. Be3, or 6. Be2. The Class B player usually adopts this line "to avoid book." He has the wrong attitude. He should book himself up extensively on this line. Instead, he avoids the study (Read: work) necessary to play this variation.

6. ..., Qc7

This is as good a choice as any. Black could play systems with 6. ..., g6; 6. ..., N8d7; 6. ..., Qb6; 6. ..., Nc6; and 6. ..., e5. The serious Class A player will select one of these systems to study. Correspondence play is an excellent way to learn such an opening.

7. Be2

A Master might say that 7. Bd3 is better as later White can play Qe2 to support e5, which is what White's position calls for. There is hardly any faulting 7. Be2, however. Why? Answer this question for yourself.

7. ..., e6

And 7. ..., e5 is only another way of playing this opening. It might be beneficial if you investigate the difference in playing style between ..., e6 and ..., e5.

8. 0-0 Be7 9. Be3 0-0 10. Nf3 (66)

White intends to attack you by e5. As a Class A player

you have to decide now between 10. ..., Nc6 and 10. ..., N8d7. Which do you choose? and why? Analyse–think it out.

10. ..., N8d7

Good Class A play–the Knight is more flexible here, keeping options open to control e5 and c5. After ..., b5 and ..., Nb6, the Knight can support d5 or go to c4. On c6, the Knight strikes d4, a square heavily in White's camp. The Knight on c6 is unlikely to find a home on b4 as White's Queen Rook Pawn hasn't moved yet. These considerations are part of the Class A player's judgment of the position that enable him to choose ..., N8d7.

11. Bd4

White is insistent on enforcing e5. Plan Black's reaction.

11. ..., b5

This is good fighting Class A chess–Black analyses that e5 is harmless and uses the tempo to further his own queenside plans. Also good was to immediately thwart White's plan with 11. ..., e5 as 12. fxe5 dxe5 13. Be3 Ng4 14. Nd5 Nxe3 15. Nxc7 Nxd1 16. Nxa8 Bc5+ with chances for both sides or a draw.

How can the Class A player choose between two good lines? we must go back to Move 1. Black's plan in the Sicilian is to outwit his opponent–let him attack and take advantage of his overextended position.

12. e5 Ng4 13. exd6 Bxd6 14. Ng5

Analyse this position. What is Black's best line?

14. ..., Nxh2?!

This is wrong. Why? After 14. ..., N4f6, Black has a safe game. Now Black must face a ferocious attack. Why is 14. ..., Nxh2 wrong? Look at the disposition of Black's forces-on the queenside, mostly undeveloped. He is not ready to attack. Where are White's?-in attacking formation. Black's Knight on h2 is too far away to influence the following battle.

15. Bd3! (67)

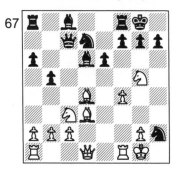

This should be a danger signal. Black's best defense is now what?

15. ..., g6?

Defense is always hard for a Class A player. The only chance to survive is 15. ..., h6 16. Bh7+ Kh8 18. Qh5 e5! Now White has a crushing retort. What is it?

16. Qel?

After 16. Qh5! you could resign. Why did both sides miss this? One reason is pattern recognition. If White had recognized this particular piece configuration around the weakened Black kingside, he might have found 16. Qh5!

How does a Class A player improve his combinational sight. One way of doing so is to study a book on tactics. These books offer an opportunity to study recurring patterns in the game. Once you "see" a move like Qh5, you should be ready to apply it in your own games.

How can such things happen: Black had a good game just moments ago. It is because Black got greedy and continued his "attack" with a single man against a well-developed enemy army. Study the early part of this game up to Move 16. Watch how Black's excellent game fell apart.

Now Black has to solve new problems.

16. ..., Nxf1

This kills an important attacker, but furies are about to occur. Can Black survive what comes next? Note White can still win by 17. Qh4 h5 18. Qxh5!

17. Nxe6?!

White *wants* to attack. He is familiar with the pattern of sacrificing a Knight on e6 to open up diagonals against Black's King, and so he plays as best he can. Look at the position after 16. ..., Nxf1. There will be a quiz later.

17. ..., fxe6

This requires calculation. Notice that Black has another defense based on his extra Rook: 17. ..., Re8. Calculate both defenses.

18. Qxe6+ Rf7 19. Bxg6

Ambitious play. White is inventive in his attacking

play, but remember he missed the crushing line earlier.

19. ..., hxg6 20. Qxg6+ Kf8 21. Qh6+

What is a defensive idea after 21. Re1? Since the open e-file is White's greatest asset, the Class A player knows how to close it to enable his King to escape.

21. ..., Ke8 22. Re1+ Kd8 23. Nd5

All White's pieces are working, but he is down three pieces. Plan Black's escape.

**23. ..., Qc6 24. Qg5+ Nf6 25. Nxf6 Rxf6
26. Qxf6+ Kc7 27. Kxf1 Bd7 (68)**

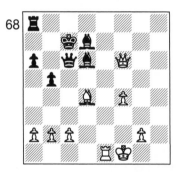

So White's attack is over. He has three Pawns for his Bishop, but his King is exposed and Black's Bishops are powerful. Black has weathered the storm and now can turn his own forces loose. This is stalwart defense, tactical defense, and adequate for a Class A player.

28. Qf7

White is still "attacking." He doesn't have the defensive skills of the Class A player.

28. ..., Rf8 29. Qg7 Rxf4+ 30. Kg1 Rg4 White Resigns

The Moral? Defend as best as you can when you have to. Your Class B opponent is more likely to go astray when the defense is tough.

Now for the quiz. Without turning back or replaying the game, set up the important elements of the position that would allow White to checkmate Black by Qh5! Can you reconstruct the tactical idea? If you can, you have added another pattern to your tactical sight. If not, go back, replay the game, and study the critical position on Move 16. Learn this pattern!

23. RUY LOPEZ
White: You
Black: 1632 Player

1. e4 e5 2. Nf3 Nc6 3. Bb5 Nf6

The Class A player knows a little something about the Berlin Defense, but why would a Class B player play it? Because he does not care to study the main lines of the Ruy Lopez. He believes his opponent is better booked. He has already conceded to you better preparation. But are you prepared to meet the Berlin Defense?

4. d3 (69)

Now the Class A player lets the tables get turned. Your opponent has already implied you are better booked than him, and now, out of a concern of being in against someone booked upon the Berlin, you select a passive line. Shame! But it's safe. Better was the standard 4. 0-0. As a Class A player, you must have faith in strong moves. The Class B player is not a Frank Marshall, sitting on a surprise innovation that will turn around the evaluation of an

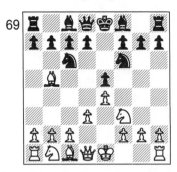

opening variation. You should respect your opponent, but not fear him. Another way of looking at it is if everybody played the Berlin against you, would you stick to 4. d3? Do not knowingly make inferior moves in the opening.

4. ..., Bc5 5. O-O Qe7

Black develops mechanically but healthily. White can forget any try to gain the advantage in the opening.

6. Nc3 Nd4 7. Ba4 c6 8. Nxd4 Bxd4

Somewhat better was 8. ..., exd4 to try to use his development, but your opponent has not shown any strong desire to gain an advantage. This lack of greed, combined with White's non-aggressive attitude, makes it difficult to win. How then will White expect to win? Answer that question.

9. Ne2

The Class A player's answer to the above question is that he will post his pieces better than Black's. At some moment, his opponent will err. Then the Class A player must become a bulldog, biting hard and hanging on. We will see...

9. ..., Bc5 10. c3 d5 11. Ng3

Again defensive minded: Black could now fully equalize by 11. ..., dxe4 12. dxe4 Bg4 13. Qe1 0-0. The Class A player knows about Pawn structure. The symmetrical Pawn structure makes winning more difficult, but this is a concommitant to 4. d3.

11. ..., Be6 12. b4?!

You know, as a Class A player, you are morally obligated in Swiss tournaments to beat your opponent. The Class A player's strength is his tactics. What is Black's tactical weakness?

12. ..., Bb6 13. exd5 Nxd5 14. Qe1

This is Black's single weakness: the unguarded e-Pawn. After 14. ..., f6, Black would stand better, but there is another weakness Black has.

14. ..., Qc7? (70)

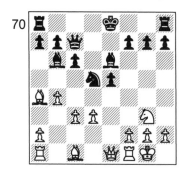

This is the other weakness: Class B players tend to respond directly to threats. He expects to have to defend. If your opponent were an Expert (plug: *How To Become a Candidate Master*) he would surely investigate 14. ..., Nxc3! 15. Qxc3 Bd4 16. Bxc6+! Bd7! with an excellent game for Black. Why does neither side see this possibility? The attitude is all. As a Class A player you *must* expect to beat your opponent. The truth of chess is hard to learn. Superior positions produce superior tactical chances.

15. c4 Bd4

You had to see this intermezzo, of course.

16. cxd5 Bxd5!

Black's best chance, giving you a chance to err. How do you save your Rook now?

17. Be3

The best–White completes his development. After 17. Rb1 Bxa2, Black picks up another Pawn.

17. ..., Bxa1 18. Qxa1 b5 19. Bb3 a5

OK, bulldog. You've bitten Black hard. You know you have winning material now. The Class D player may equate B+N=R+P, but as a Class A player you know you are winning. How do you begin to sue your plus?

20. Qc3

This is all right, but the Class A player's by-word is attack. As an attacker, you would like to keep Black's King in the center of the board. The bulldog would bite deeper with 20. Bxd5 cxd5 21. Bc5 axb4 22. Bxb4. Class A players should take every opportunity to find the attacking line.

20. ..., Bxb3 21. axb3 0-0 22. Rc1 f5

Black sends fighters out. How serious is Black's attack? Analyse.

23. Bc5 Rf6 24. Re1!

White shifts his attack to Black's center and a collapse is eminent. This is good Class A play. If now 24. ..., Rae8, White can choose between 25. f4 and 25. d4, e4 26. f3.

24. ..., axb4 25. Qxb4 f4 26. Ne4 Re6 (71)

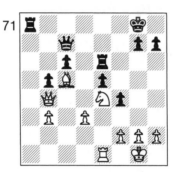

How should White proceed? Analyse.

27. Ng5! Rg6 28. h4 h6 29. Qe4!

Neatly played. You must be able to see such ideas. If you failed to find this line, go back to Move 26. Visualize the position. Run it through in your mind, not on the board. Class A players are attackers, and the tactical world is their home. They must be able to see tactics. For this reason, learning to play a single game blindfolded is good practice in visualization. If you have a friend who is patient, try it with him. You should set up the stipulation that an illegal move on your part constitutes a loss. Don't give up if you find it difficult; it is designed to improve your perception of the board, not to "show off."

29. ..., hxg5 30. Qxg6 gxh4 31. Bd6

The end is approaching. Once the three White forces gang up on Black's King, it will be all over.

**31. ..., Qa5 31. Qe6+ Kh7 32. Rxe5 Qa1+
33. Kh2 g6 34. Qf7+ Kh6 35. Bf8+ Black Resigns**

24. CENTER COUNTER GAME
White: You
Black: 1634 Player

1. e4 d5 2. exd5 Nf6 3. Nc3

Comment upon this move.

3. ..., Nxd5 4. Bc4 e6

White's idea behind 3. Nc3 becomes clear after 4. ...,
Nxc3 5. Qf3! e6 6. Qxc3 with a good game for White.

5. Nf3 (72)

White had several choices here–5.N1e2 keeping his
Pawn structure sound and 5. Qe2 to reply dxc3 promoting
rapid development. White's doubled Pawns will be
compensated for by his lead in development. Three tempi
are worth a Pawn. Two tempi are worth doubled Pawns.

124

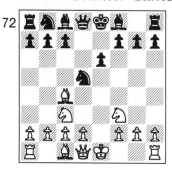

5. ..., Nxc3 6. bxc3 Bd6

The square e5 will be contested. Black is about equal here. Why?

7. d4 Nd7 8. 0-0 Nf6

Black willingly forfeits the battle for e5, and for what? A vague sense of King safety. Class A players are not as likely to give up a sound plan. Better was 8. ..., 0-0 9. Re1 (overprotecting e5) b6 and Black's Bishop finds a healthy diagonal. Black will continue with ..., Bb7, ..., c5, and, if necessary, ..., Qc7 and ..., e5 with a good game–the realization of his plan begun with 6. ..., Bd6.

9. Bg5

You, on the other hand, can pursue your plan of using your superior development to conquer the square Black gave up. The pin with Bg5 will eventually require Black to retreat further with ..., Be7 to break it.

9. ..., a6

Black looks for counterplay with queenside expansion, but White's reply only gives White more space there. Better was 9. ..., 0-0.

10. a4 0-0 (73)

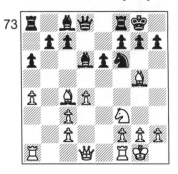

We have discussed White's plan. What is White's best way to begin? Black's position is sound–there are no immediate weaknesses. Once you have your own plan in mind (Re1, Ne5, and Qf3 to pressure Black's kingside, you can take the time to see what Black's best counterplan may be. If Black varies from your analysis of his best line, it helps you to take advantage of his inferior line.

11. Re1 Re8?!

This does not answer the requirements of the position–e5 is not a square easily within Black's control and f7 is weakened. Black might have tried 11. ..., b6 12. Ne5 Bb7 as the tactical greediness of 13. Bxf6?! Qxf6 14. Nd7 is punished by 14. ..., Qh4! with a decisive attack (work it out!)

12. Ne5 Be7 13. Qf3 c6

You have improved your position, and Black's game remains passive. What is next in your plan?

14. Rad1

There were three, perhaps four, candidate moves in the position. Let us consider them from the point of view of the Class A player.

126

A) 14. a5. This is a "binding" move, but after 14. ..., Qc7, Black's Queen supports the freeing ...., c5 and White's Rook is tied down to protecting a5. White's position is strong, but he was thinking kingside attack a move ago. To suddenly get ambitious for a board-wide bind is an overplay.

B) 14. Re2. Designed to double on the e-file, but since the e-file will remain closed, it is doubtful two Rooks belong on the file.

C) 14. Bd3. This play contains the immediate threat of 15. Bxf6 Bxf6 16. Bxh7+! Kxh7 17. Qh5+ Kg8 18. Qxf7+ Kh7 19. Re3 Bg5 20. Rh3+ Bh6 21. Rxh6+ Kxh6 22. Qg6 mate. Black's best defense to 14. Bd3 is 14. ..., Rf8.

D) 14. Rad1. The Class A player is not without guile. He makes ..., c5 more difficult, and Bd3 may come in later when it looks more like White is retreating (after an eventual ..., b5)

Of the choices, 14. Rad1 is good Class A play.

14. ..., Rf8!?

And this is good Class B defense, much better than the "automatic developing" response of 14. ..., Bd7.

15. Bd3 Nd5

Seeking simplification is Black's proper strategy. What is White to do?

16. Qh5!?

Commendable aggression–A Master would try 16. Bxe7 Qxe7 17. c4 Nf6 18. c5! when the squares d6 and b6 are weak and White has a solid advantage. Defense, however, is not the Class B player's forte. Best for Black after 16. Qh5!? is the difficult to find 16. ..., g6 17. Bxe7 (analyze that 17. Nxg6 is not adequate) Qxe7 18. Qh6 f6 and Black can defend. A Class B player might fall into this defense but would be unlikely to plan it.

16. ..., f5?! (74)

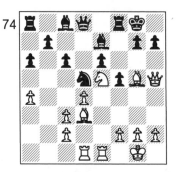

What is White's best method of attacking Black's position? Analyse. Do not move the pieces–think!

17. h4?!

Not too bad–White remains aggressive. Retreat by 17. Bd2 to avoid exchanging pieces is probably best. After 17. Bxe7 Qxe7 18. c4 Nf6, White's attack has ended.

17. ..., Bxg5?!

The Class B player declines the offered Pawn–17. ..., Nxc3 would force White to demonstrate he has something for his Pawn. The Class B opponent is not an expert, however. He can be intimidated. His King's house is on fire. He is thinking immediate defense, not a distant Pawn plus ending. Is this a matter of luck or constant pressure? We will leave the conclusion to you.

18. hxg5 Nf4 19. Qh4 Ng6

Black seeks to exchange White's aggressive Knight. Analyse the continuation after 19. ..., Nxd3.

20. Nxg6

After 19. ..., Nxd3 20. Rxd3 Qe7 21. Rh3 g6 22. Nxg6! is a winner.

20. ..., hxg6 (75)

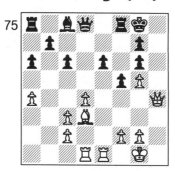

What are White's advantages? Disadvantages? Plans?

21. g4

White properly continues to attack. This is healthy Class A play. Also good was 21. Re3 and Rh3 to invade on h7.

21. ..., b5

At last, counterplay! but Black is already seriously compromised on the other side of the board.

22. Re3 Qd5 23. Rh3 Bd7 24. Qh7+ Kf7 25. Rh6! (76)

The invasion of Black's position is complete. Death and destruction follow. This is the result of White's consistent, aggressive attitude.

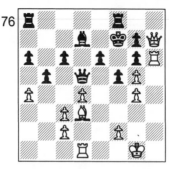

25. ..., Be8 26. gxf5!

Opening up fatal lines. Remember, White is hunting a King, not Pawns. After 26. Qxg6+ Ke7 27. Qxg7+ Rf7, Black could organize a defense of sorts. Now 26. ..., gxf5 fails to what? Analyse.

26. ..., exf5

After 26. ..., gxf5 27. Rf6+! Ke7 28. Qxg7+ Rf7 29. Rxf7+ Bxf7 30. g6 wins.

27. Re1!

White uses all his forces. The end is near.

27. ..., Qd8

Of course, 27. ..., Qd6 28. Bxf5 is fatal.

28. Qxg6+ Kg8 29. Qh7+ Kf7 30. Rf6+ Black Resigns

25. CATALAN OPENING
White: You
Black: 1611 Player

1. d4 Nf6 2. c4 e6 3. Nc3 b6

The Class A player is obviously aware that this move normally occurs after 3. Nf3. Why should the Class A player refrain from 4. e4 ? No reason other than a desire to play "book." We have seen this twisted reasoning before. The Class A player should be happy to leave book.

4. Nf3 Bb7 5. g3

Happy?

131

5. ..., d5

And Black still doesn't want to play a Queen's Indian Defense. Now if White is also well booked on the Catalan, his decision on move four was still poor. The fact is that Class A players must realize that they are almost always better prepared and better chess players than their Class B opponent, but relying on superior preparation simply postpones the original part of the game. As long as his opponent plays book, he has the accumulated wisdom (and therefore safety) of many Masters behind him. The sooner the battle actually starts, the more likely the Class A player is to exert his strength.

6. Bg2 dxc4 7. 0-0 Be7 8. Qa4+ N8d7
9. Qxc4 a6 10. Bf4 c5 11. dxc5 Bxc5 (77)

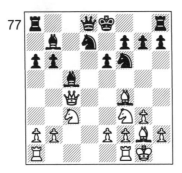

Now what advantage does White have? Analyse and comment.

12. a4

White's edge is very slight. He has a two-move (0-0 and Qc4) advantage on Black. He will be able to occupy the d-file first. This should be White's plan.

12. ..., 0-0 13. Rfd1 Qc8

How should White meet the threat of 14. ..., Bxf2+ ?

14. e3

This requires close calculation. What is Black's best? Analyse.

14. ..., Ng4?!

This carries the threat of 15. ..., Nxf2! 16. Kxf2 Bxe3+. But tactics arise from superior positions, not inferior ones. White can play 15. b4! Be7 16. Qxc8 Bxc8 (else Rxd7) 17. Bd6 and White has gained space. Black cannot try 15. b4! Bxe3 16. Qxc8 Bxf2+ 17. Kf1 Bxc8 18. h3 Ne3+ 19. Kxf2 Nxd1+ 20. Rxd1 with the advantage.

Class A players should work to improve their tactics. Play over these lines in your head. Visualize them until their conclusion.

15. Qd3

White opts for another sound plan–the pressure of the open d-file.

15. ..., Bc6

More in the style of Class A play is 15. ..., Rd8 to contest the d-file, but your opponent is a Class B player– he makes direct defenses, not a cohesive plan of defense.

16. Ng5!

Threat: mate

16. ..., N7f6

Analyse how White wins a Pawn after 16. ..., N4f6.

17. h3 Bxg2 18. Kxg2 Qc6+ 19. Kg1 h6 (78)

What happens on 19. ..., Nh6 ? Analyse. A Class A player should find 19. Be5 Nf5 20. g4 h6 21. Nxf7 Rxf7 22. gxf5 with the advantage.

20. hxg4?!

Here our Class A player slips. This is OK–he can't see everything. The important thing is that he tries to. After 20. N5e4! White will win a Pawn or open up the Black kingside.

20. ..., hxg5 21. Bxg5 Nxg4 22. Qe2 Ne5 23. e4

The position is equal. After 23. ..., f6, how does White proceed?

23. ..., f6 24. Be3

The Class A player should never be afraid to simplify when he has to. By exchanging Black's strong Bishop, White cuts down on Black's attacking chances. Though the endgame is not the Class A player's forte, he is usually better off than the Class B player there.

24. ..., Bxe3 25. Qxe3 Nc4 26. Qe2 Qc5

Black should be planning to occupy the d-file. This is shilly-shallying.

27. Rd7 Ne5 28. R7d1

You should not be interested in a draw (28. Rd2 Nc4) in such a position. The position may be even, but you are a better player than your opponent.

28. ..., g6?!

This is the reason you should not be content with a draw. The text weakens Black's kingside. Better was 28. ..., Rfd8 as 29. Rxd8 Rxd8 30. Qxa6 Rd2 is very strong for Black, but Black finds it hard to leave his a-Pawn "unprotected." The weakness of the Class B player coming to the fore: Class A players always think aggressively.

29. Rac1 Qe7 30. Rd2 Qh7?!

Black still could try 30. ..., Rfd8. On h7 the Queen is in danger of getting out of play.

31. f4 Nf7 32. Qe3 (79)

Left on his own, Black has nearly ruined his position. Now he lets his b-Pawn go and White wins. Bad play? Typical.

32. ..., Nh6 33. Qxb6 Qf7 34. R1d1

Now White dominates the d-file and the end is close.

Notice how White outplays Black in the simpler ending play.

34. ..., Rae8

Letting go another Pawn for what? The Class A player analyses, finds the a-Pawn healthy, and eats.

35. Qxa6 Ra8 36. Qe2 Qa7+ 37. Kg2 Qb7 38. Rd7

The end is rapidly approaching.

38. ..., Qb3 39. Rc7 Rf7 40. Rxf7 Nxf7 41. Rd2

Solid play. The two queenside Pawns must win.

41. ..., Rc8 42. Qb5 Rb8
43. Qxb3 Rxb3 44. a5 g5 45. a6 Rb8 46. b4

And it is all over.

46. ..., Kf8 47. b5 Ke7 48. a7 Ra8 49. b6 Nd8

Finish him off.

50. Rxd8 Kxd8 51. b7 Black Resigns

26. SICILIAN DEFENSE
White: 1758 Player
Black: You

1. e4 c5 2. Nf3 d6 3. Be2

This passive-looking move can easily transpose into standard lines–3. ..., Nf6 4. Nc3 e6 5. d4 cxd4 6. Nxd4, etc. This could be sophisticated opening play (unlikely–see the discussion in the previous game) or an attempt to take you out of the books. What is your reaction? What is your plan? Yes, game plans can be laid as early as Move 3.

3. ..., Nf6 4. Nc3 g6

A good line for the Class A player to adopt. White cannot easily find a vicious line against the Dragon with his Bishop on e2. His next move indicates a passive attitude–as we have seen, a common failing of the Class B player.

5. h3 Bg7 6. d3

Now we are out of the Open Sicilian (for a while

137

anyway) and Black has to begin to lay some further plans to develop his pieces. Castle is obvious.

6. ..., Nc6 7. Be3 Rb8

Planning to undertake a queenside expansion. Also good is 7. ..., 0-0. The Class A player, of course, is familiar with the space-gaining maneuver ..., b5. How is he familiar with the idea? By playing over Master games in the openings he likes to play.

8. Qd2 b5 9. a3

Further instances of the passive play that occasionally infects a Class B player. This will not stop your opening up the queenside, but will aid it. Better was 9. 0-0.

9. ..., a5 10. d4?!

On the principle that the best way to combat flank play is to open up the center, but this constitutes a lost tempo (6. d3, 10. d4) and weakens e4.

10. ..., b4 (80)

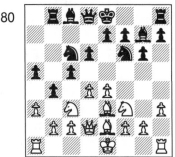

Of course. As a Class A player, do you expect to win this game? Explain.

11. axb4 cxb4

This is OK, but better is 11. ..., axb with continued pressure on White's center. Why should Black violate general rules (capture toward the center) to punish White's passive play? The Class A player should know better, but from time to time he will go astray.

12. Bb5

Another lost tempo-the Class B player plans for the immediate solution, but his game is horrible. Plan to take advantage of White's misplays. **(81)**

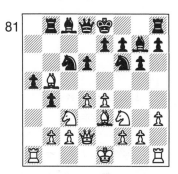

12. ..., Bb7?!

This allows unnecessary complications. After 13. d5! bxc3 14. Qxc3 0-0! 15. dxc6 Nxe4 16. Qxa5 Qxa5 17. Rxa5, there is still a fight. The Class A player likes complications, but when none are needed, sound play is better-12. ..., Bd7 prevented all this.

13. Bxc6+?! Bxc6 14. Ne2 Nxe4

And you have broken White's center. Victory seems eminent, but chess is not a simple game. A Master would be expected to win this position. A Class A player has to find good moves and a solid plan.

15. Qd3

What is White's threat? How do you meet it?

15. ..., Nf6

Good play, stopping d5 and keeping threats of ..., Bb5 and ..., Bxf3 in the air.

16. Bd2 0-0 17. Ng3 Qc7

Why does the Queen go here? What is Black's long range plan? Is c2 weak?

18. c4

Evaluate this move.

18. ..., bxc3 19. Bxc3 a4 20. d5 (82)

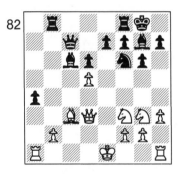

Analyse this surprise play.

20. ..., Nxd5

Surprise moves need to be carefully calculated. Here the Class A player can easily calculate that 20. d5 is without merit and properly takes the extra Pawn. At lower levels (Class C) players often take first. That is not Class A chess. Note that if Black plays 20. ..., Bxd5, White responds with 21. Rxa4, and not the unfavorable 21. Bxf6? Bc4!

21. Bxg7 Kxg7 22. 0-0 (83)

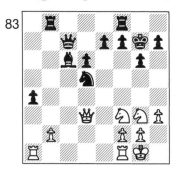

Analyse. What is Black's plan?

22. ..., Kg8

Not a bad move, but not a Class A move. Class A players should always be thinking *attack*. With 22. ..., Nf4! Black conjures up threats of ..., Nxg2, ..., Nxh3+ and (maybe) ..., Ne2+. The Knight is perfectly safe–23. Qe3 e5 and Black threatens the devastating ..., Rb3. Why 22. ..., Kg8 ? After eating a hearty meal of two Pawns, Black would like to take a nap and wake up with 1-0 on the score sheet. Class A players have to win their games, and aggressive play is the best way to do it. Subtract 20 rating points for 22. ..., Kg8.

23. Rfc1 Qb7 24. Qc4 Bb5 25. Qh4

Notice how your failure to attack on Move 22 has allowed White to gain a preponderance of forces on the kingside. The Class A player is not likely to see when stern defensive measures are necessary. This is excusable.

25. ..., Nf6

This is an adequate move. An expert might select ...., f6. Why?

26. Ng5 Rfc8

After 26. ..., Bc6, Black guards the critical e4 square.

27. N3e4 h5 28. Nxf6+ exf6 29. Ne4 Rxc1 30. Rxc1 (84)

Plan? Notice how Black's two extra Pawns (shortly to be one) have lost value. Review the game from Moves 22 on to see how this happened.

30. ..., Bd3?!

Criticize this move. Do not touch the pieces. Analyse. What was better?

31. Nxf6+

After 30. ..., f5 31. Nxd6 Qd5! Black had every expectation of still winning even though only heavy pieces may be left on the board.

31. ..., Kg7?

This, however, is a blunder. With 31. ..., Kf8, White's attack is not sufficient. Why? This is an example of a blunder that is not fully controllable by the Class A player. The game has taken an unexpected turn with his opponent putting up stern resistance. Without analysing ..., Kf8, the Class A player plays the "automatic" ..., Kg7 and suffers the consequences. Class B players can play chess and should not be taken lightly.

32. Nxh5+! gxh5 33. Qd4+ Kg8
34. Qxd3 Qxb2 35. Qg3+ Kh8 36. Qc3+

The Class B player gets excited, too. With 36. Rc7!? the game remains wide open. Instead he seeks salvation in a Rook and Pawn ending–not a bad choice as endgames are much harder to play than middle games.

36. ..., Qxc3 37. Rxc3 (85)

A plan for Black?

37. ..., Ra8

Correct–Rooks belong behind passed Pawns.

38. Ra3 Kg7

And Kings belong in the center.

39. Kf1 Kf6 40. Ke2 Ke5 41. Kd3 Kd5
42. Kc3 Kc5 43. Kb2 (86)

Eventually White must retreat. He does so immediately

rather than weaken his kingside Pawn structure. Stern play!

43. ..., Kb4 44. Rf3 a3+ 45. Ka2 Ra7 46. Rf5 Rc7

So far, Black has played the endgame well. Should Black win from this position?

47. Rf4+ Rc4 48. Rxf7

The Class A player should recognize the ending is lost after 48. Rxc4+. This is not calculation but a familiarity with basic endings. This familiarity can be gained by studying endgame books or the endgame column (by Pal Benko) in *Chess Life.* If you cannot verbalize how Black wins after 48. Rxc4+, you need to take the time to study an endgame book on King and Pawn endings. The classic is *Basic Chess Endings* by Reuben Fine.

48. ..., Rc2+ 49. Kal d5

Proper play. What does White play next?

50. g4 hxg4 51. hxg4 d4 52. Rb7+ Kc3
53. Rc7+ Kd2 54. Rd4 d3 55. g5

Does Black have a win? Analyse.

55. ..., Ke2 56. g6 d2 57. g7 Rcl+

Here is where the Class A player fails–after 57. ..., Rc8! 58. Re7+ Kd1 59. f4 Kc2 60. Rd7 d1(Q)+ 61. Rxd1 Kxd1 62. f5 Kc2 (threat ..., Kb3) 63. Ka2 Kc3 64. f6 Kb4 65. f7 Rc2+ 66. Kb1 Kb3, Black mates. This is high class endgame play, the province of the Master. Sometimes Class B opponents play a Class A game. Endgames are difficult for the Class A player, Experts, and Masters. The Class A player should look for earlier decisions unless there is nothing better.

58. Ka2 Rg1 59. Re7+ Kxf2 60. Rf7+ Ke3 DRAWN

Class B players should never be taken lightly...

27. SICILIAN DEFENSE
White: You
Black: 1626 Player

1. e4 c5 2. c3

The popularity of the Alapin Variation is perplexing. Class A players would do better to stick to the more open game starting with 2. Nf3. The center play and tactics should be more to his style than the "positional" 2. c3.

2. ..., d5

Black chooses to open up the game. Chessically, this is not a bad choice. Practically, Black would be better off with the quieter 2. ..., Nf6.

3. exd5 Qxd5 4. Na3

This is something of an innovation, but it doesn't have enough to recommend it over the standard 4. d4. Why does the Class A player vary here? We have answered that question several times before. It does have the virtue that Black is now out of his own book.

4. ..., Nf6 5. Nf3 e6

The Class B player prepares to develop his pieces. He doesn't think like a Class A player. The Class A player plays 5. ..., Bg4. The Class B player rejects 5. ..., Bg4 because of 6. Be2 and Black won't be able to play ..., Bxf3 as Bxf3 will drive Black's Queen away. The Class A player looks at White's thematic move, d4. With the Knight on a3, White does not have the follow-up of Nc3. Therefore, any move that weakens White's grip over d4 must favor Black. Best was 5. ..., Bg4.

6. d4 a6

Black rejects the natural 6. ..., cxd4 because of 7. Nb5, but is this so bad for Black? After 7. ..., Na6 8. N3xd4 Be7, Black is no worse than White.

7. Nc4 Qd8

This is a good play–the Queen is awkwardly placed on d5 after 7. ..., N8d7. By retreating now, Black saves himself tactical headaches later. Class B players can make good moves, this is undeniable. The difference is in the aggressive quality of the moves: Class A players seek action, aggression. Class B players seek comfort.

8. a4 b6

This is the comfort of which we spoke. Black could seek rapid development and allow White to expand on the queenside–while he is almost undeveloped. After 8. ..., Be7 9. a5 N8d7 10. Be2 0-0 11. 0-0 b5! 12. axb6 Nxb6 13. dxc5 Bxc5 14. Qxd8 Rxd8 15. Nxb6 Bxb6 and though White has a protected passed c-Pawn, he does not have the advantage. It is not expected that the Class B player could calculate this. The point is that he looks for "comfort"

The Class A player looks for a (favorable) fight.

9. Qb3 N8d7 10. Bf4 Be7 11. dxc5

You see that 11. Nd6+ isn't quite adequate. If not, analyse 11. Nd6+ Bxd6 12. Bxd6 Ne4 13. Bf4 Bb7 14. Bd3 0-0 and Black's game is OK. As always, analyse it in your head. White's plan is to bring another piece to bear on d6, but his development needs catching up so Black's d6 is relatively safe–for now.

11. ..., Bxc5 12. Rd1 0-0 13. Be2 Bb7 14. 0-0 Bd5!

Nicely played. The Class B player is aware of the concept of centralization. The situation is very tense.

15. Qc2 (87)

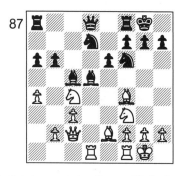

White is right in retreating. This leaves Black some pleasant choices: 15. ..., Be4 or 15 ..., Nh5 (to drive the Bishop off the h2-b8 diagonal, especially d6) or ..., Ne4. Surprisingly, Black selects none of these. Why? Black's "solution" is typical Class B play: he threatens to win a Pawn by 15. ..., Rc8 with the threat of ..., Bxc4 and ..., Bxf2+. The fight has been over d6 and the central squares. His 14. ..., Bd5 was played to shield this square. Now he ups the ante in the battle over d6. This move could be very good played by a Master. But a Master has a different reasoning behind ..., Rc8.

15. ..., Rc8!? 16. Nd6

The Class A player is willing to do hand-to-hand combat. At the moment, the calculation of the position is beyond both players. This is in favor of the Class A player. He may not be able to calculate to the end of the fight, but he is able to calculate better. This ability to calculate can be learned. It comes from natural ability or practice. If you want to play Class A chess, you must improve your ability to calculate.

16. ..., Rc6 17. Nb7 Qa8 18. Nxc5 Nxc5
19. Nd4 R6c8 20. Bd6

OK, analyse! After 20. ..., Rfd8, how does White meet the threats of ..., Rxd6 and ..., Bxg2 ?

You must be able to find the tactical trick: 20. ..., Rfd8 21. Be7 Bxg2?! 22. Bxd8 Bxf1 23. Bf3! Why *must* you be able to find this? It is the will of the Class A player to win. Bobby Fischer (Remember him? His birthday is March 9. Send him a birthday card: Robert Fischer, PO Box 50307, Pasadena, California 91105.) talked about cracking the will of the other player. You must be as resolute. Search every complicated position for a winning try. When you analyse a position as good for your opponent, try looking just one move farther to see if there is a "turn-around" move. If you do that here, you may find Bf3.

20. ..., Bxg2

Safe is 20. ..., Rfe8, with rough equality. The Class B player hasn't seen the "trick." Will is a terrible thing.

21. Bxf8 Bh3?

Even after the better 21. ..., Bxf1 22. Bf3! Qb8 23. Bxc5

bxc5 24. Nc6, White is winning, but 21. ..., Be4! 22. Qd2 Kxf8 leaves Black with plenty of chances due to the weakened White kingside. The Class B player is too intent on simplistic plans.

22. Bf3 Qb8 23. Bxc5 bxc5

White is a Rook ahead almost like magic. This was not accidental. Black became discouraged in the fight, his will sapped, he did not follow the program of the game. The glitch produced a negative Rook.

24. Nc6 Rxc6 25. Bxc6 Ng4

The last hurrah...

26. f3 Ne3 27. Qd2 Nxd1 28. Rxd1 Kf8
29. Qd8+ Qxd8 30. Rxd8+ Ke7 31. Ra8 Black Resigns

This is an interesting game to go back over. Black fights well for awhile, but fades at the end: the cracking of wills is not an accidental thing. Notice how the Class A player is constantly trying to boss the action.

28. ALEKHINE'S DEFENSE
White: 1635 Player
Black: You

1. e4 Nf6 2. d3

This is a good line against the Alekhine Defense if that is what the Class B player usually plays. If the line is played out of fear, however, then it is not as good as the standard 2. e5.

2. ..., e5 3. Nf3 Nc6 4. c3

Already a slight error. Better is 4. g3 to fianchetto the King Bishop. Why is the Bishop better on g2 than e2? On g2 it supports the e-Pawn and indirectly pressures d5. On e2 the Bishop is passive, only. The Class A player (you) needs to know how to combat White's passive play. What do you do now?

4. ..., d5

Of course! Black reacts strongly in the center. This is all standard stuff, but notice how powerful the "standard stuff" can be.

5. N1d2

White knows the general outlines of handling this system: keep the center locked, protect e4, and prepare the fianchetto, but that tempo with 4. c3 creates a problem. As an exercise, how can you best prevent White from properly locating his white squared Bishop?

5. ..., Bg4!?

If you found this line to prevent 6. g3, bravo! You have the makings of a strong player. Why is 6. g3 prevented? Analyse. Find it!

6. Be2

White cannot play 6. g3 as 6. ..., dxe4 7. dxe4 Nxe4! 8. Nxe4 Qxd1+ 9. Kxd1 Bxf3+ wins.

6. ..., Bc5 7. 0-0 0-0 8. exd5 Nxd5 9. Nxe5!? (88)

Such moves can be very disconcerting in a tournament game. Black has to decide if it's good or not and the calculations can be tough. As a practical method, you should first find a safe line and then look for something better.

9. ..., Bxe2

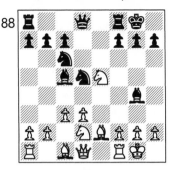

The safe line is 9. ..., Nxe5 10. Bxg4 Nxd3. Analyse which is better.

10. Qxe2

White cannot continue with 10. Nxc6 Qe8! when White loses material. Black dug in to find 9. ..., Bxe2! on the theory that combinations don't work from inferior positions (White's).

10. ..., Nf4 11. Qe4 Nxe5 12. Qxe5 Nxd3

And Black keeps his lead in development and regains the Pawn. This is how you should strive to play: be alert, make your opponent pay for his sins. **(89)**

13. Qg3?

Only by 13. Qe2 Re8 14. Qd1 could White avoid

the immediate loss of a piece, but Black obviously has a strong attack.

13. ..., Nxc1 14. Raxc1 Qxd2

By simple means you have established a winning game. Your next step is to win that game. Your extra piece should start toward White's King. You can afford even exchanges, your opponent can't.

15. Qxc7 Bxf2+ 16. Kh1 Rae8

This is the proper idea: use your forces to attack White. Forget about those foot soldiers on the queenside–they can't reach White's King.

17. Rcd1 Qxb2 18. Qf4 Re2 19. Qf3

Comment on 19. ..., Bb6.

19. ..., Qxa2

This play is good–it protects the one weak link in Black's setup, the square f7. Note how unfamiliarity with a tactical trap could cost Black all his fine strategy: 19. ..., Be3? 20. Qxf7+! and White mates, but on 19. ..., Bb6, the square d8 is guarded so the mate doesn't work.

20. Qxb7 h6 21. Qf3 R8e8 22. h3 Bb6 23. Qg4

Your job now is to put away the White King. What's the procedure?

23. ..., Rf2!

This is the simplest: exchange off a piece or two as the ending is an easy win.

24. c4 Rxf1+ 25. Rxf1 Qe2 26. Qf4 Qe6 27. Qc1 Bc7

And the Bishop relocates on a deadlier diagonal. All this is the Class A player's "technique" and is worth study.

28. Rf3? Qe1+ 29. Qxe1 Rxe1+ White Resigns

29. KING'S GAMBIT
White: You
Black: 1634 Player

1. e4 e5 2. f4

The King's Gambit went through a period of time when it was "refuted." The refutation was published in the *American Chess Bulletin* by one Robert James Fischer. It was an impressive argument and soon the King's Gambit was as scarce as fleas on a snake. That Fischer had lost earlier on the Black side of a King's Gambit to Boris Spassky seemed forgotten. The Chess God had spoken...

A number of years has passed since Fischer's pronouncement, and every so often a King's Gambit is seen. The opening is not yet dead. Class A players can use this opening. It is ideal for them as it is an open game with definite tactical themes in it. Since the heart of the Class A player's game is attack, let us watch this game and comment.

2. ..., exf4

By the same token, the Class B player would be better off declining by 2. ..., Bc5 or counter-gambitting by 2. ..., d5.

3. Nf3 Be7 4. Bc4 Bh4+ 5. Kf1

Black has selected the Cunningham Defense to the King's Gambit. For his negative Pawn and loss of castling, White has superior development and the better center and an awkwardly posted Black Bishop. Chances are about even, but the position is not. This should make the Class A player happy. Are you happy with White? Why or why not? Analyse the position. See if you can determine what your "feel" is for the position after Move 5.

5. ..., Be7

Black is failing to use the knowledge that Class B players have but do not use. The best way to play against a gambit is to return the material for your own rapid development. With 5. ..., d5! Black keeps his game healthy. The Class A player should be more than familiar with this idea: he should use it. In this position, 5. ..., d5 should be your first choice of defense.

6. Nc3 c6 7. d4 b5?!

Notice the difference between a Class A player and a Class B player. Black thinks he is driving the White pieces out of the center. Watch where they end up in a few moves. Yet he is neglecting the center himself, and White soon dominates there. Check for yourself how much better 7. ..., Nf6!? 8. e5 Nh5!? or 8. Bxf4 d5! is. At least then Black could fight on even terms.

Analyse now–where does White's Bishop belong, on b3 or d3? Answer: on b3. Why? Because it is still attacking f7 on b3 while on d3 it is somewhat passive.

157

8. Bd3 b4 9. Ne2 g5

Black, who has nearly no development is expanding on both sides of the board while the center remains in White's control. Now you, as White, must come up with some plan to use your center. What is your idea?

10. d5

You had to choose between 10. d5 and 10. e5. Which one is better? It is hard for the Class A player to make this judgment, but he probably should have selected 10. e5!? as it cramps Black's kingside since the Pawn on c6 already interferes with his Knight and Bishop. The Class A player may have rejected 10. e5 as 10. ..., g4 forces 11. Nd2 and congestion, but this is not quite true. From d2 the Knight can spring to e4 when Black's advanced Pawns are very weak. The Class A player needs to press himself when choosing between two lines of play to look just a little deeper.

10. ..., h5?! (90)

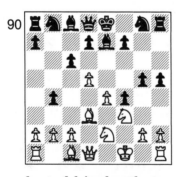

Black has neglected his development. How can you take advantage of this? It should be in the repertoire of a Class A player to know the standard attack against Black's King's Gambit kingside: with 11. h4! the Pawn formation is thrown into disharmony. The Pawn on f4 will die, and

White's center will be secure. Black may gain the Pawn on h4, but this will open the h-file and this is a gain for White.

How does White know all this? By studying Master games based on the King's Gambit. If you are going to play 2. f4, you should at least look at some of the classic old games to note how they progressed. *In studying to become a Class A player, it is more important to study games played from Morphy to Lasker than games from Capablanca to Kasparov. The old games will reveal more about fundamentals than the newer games.*

But you want to play modern chess? Don't worry, the older games are the basis of modern chess. Learn the fundamentals: the rest will come from this.

11. c4?!

This is not a bad idea, strengthening his center. The ?! is just for not finding h4!

11. ..., c5 12. Qa4

White is having a difficult time in this game because he is not familiar with how h4! works against Black's kingside. Book knowledge is not just memorizing opening variations: it is knowing the patterns of procedure in analogous positions. White wants to stir up some action but he doesn't know how as 12. e5 is met by ..., d6 and White's center attack comes to a halt. Now he threatens e5 because of the pin on d7, but the Queen is out of place on a4. The Class A player knows this but it is development and fits in with his plan.

It is true that a bad plan is better than no plan at all. Black has not had a consistent plan; White has.

12. ..., g4?!

OK, your move.

13. Ne1

White rejects, correctly, 13. Ne5, Bf6 14. Bxf4 Qe7 15. d6 Qe6! and Black wins the ambitious Knight. This is a matter of calculation, and you *must* be able to see this. If not, run it over again in your head. Practice mental calculation until you can see three or four moves ahead.

13. ..., Qc7?!

Since the f-Pawn is doomed, a Class A player would opt to destroy White's Pawn cover by 13. ..., f3!?

14. Bxf4 Bd6 15. g3 h4 16. Kg2 h3+ 17. Kf2 (91)

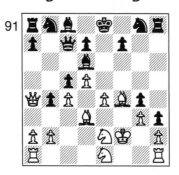

Note how the battle has gone. Black still has space on both flanks; but White's development has increased and his center is strong. White is winning this war. His consistent strategy, though not necessarily the best, was better than Black's policy of Pawn moves only. This is what is meant by "Class A players play better chess than Class B players." Class A players stick to the general principles better than Class B players, and they select their moves based on the requirements of their plan.

17. ..., Bxf4 18. gxf4!

Now White's center takes on the aspect of an impending avalanche. The square g3 becomes available for a Knight, and the base of Black's space (g4) will come under attack. Strategically, White has a won game.

18. ..., Nh6 19. Nc2 0-0

There is no happiness in this house. Black castles because he could never figure out how to break the pin on his d-Pawn. He could have tried 18. ..., Bb7 and ..., Na6, and ..., 0-0-0.

20. Rag1 d6

Finally! but Black's game is already too seriously compromised.

21. Ne3 Qe7 22. Rg3 Qf6 23. Rhg1 Qh4

Black's defense is a move-for-move one. He has had no consistent plan to safeguard his King. White's threat of Rxh3 finds Black going over to complete defense. Notice how all of White's pieces are kingside bound but one. When the Queen comes into the fray, it will be all over. For that reason, a Class A attacker might think about 24. Bb1 and Qc2 to follow.

24. Ke1

White's plan is obviously to unpin by Kd2.

24. ..., Nd7 25. Qc6?! Rb8
26. Kd2 Kh8 27. Nxg4 Rb6 (92)

28. Nxh6!

A very nice sacrifice that shows the Class A player at

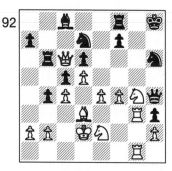

his best. Acceptance is fatal–28. ..., Rxc6 29. Nxf7+! Rxf7
30. Rg8+ Kh7 31. e5+ Kh6 32. Rh8+ Rh7 33. Rxh7 mate

28. ..., Qxh6 29. Qa4

When the Queen gets back into the attack...but we have
heard that note before.

29. ..., Rb7 30. Qc2 Nf6 31. b3

Finally! White's Queen will take the a1-h8 diagonal
and the end will be sudden. Black could try his hand at
resistance only by 31. ..., Rg8.

**31. ..., Nh5? 32. Qb2+ f6 33. Rg6 Qh7
34. e5 f5 35. e6+ Ng7 36. R1g5 Kg8 (93)**

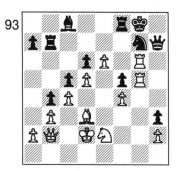

Now you must find the *coup de grâce*–how is Black to
be put away?

37. Ng3!

This is good attacking technique–White's last inactive piece is brought into the fray and it's all over.

37. ..., Kh8 38. Rh5 Qxh5 39. Nxh5 Black Resigns

White attacked consistently and well throughout this game. He may have missed the best continuation from time to time, but he was always in the fight, always pressing: good Class A play!

30. BENKO'S COUNTER GAMBIT
White: You
Black: 1652 Player

1. d4 Nf6 2. c4 c5 3. d5 b5

This is a good opening choice for your opponent to play against you. The Benko Counter Gambit makes it difficult for White to attack: he is in possession of an extra Pawn on a2, far from the scene of battle. Black's pieces usually become quite active.

How should the Class A player procede? He should take the Pawn and learn to try to make it useful. It is a method of play in advance of the skills of most Class A

164

players, but it is a valuable skill as one approaches Expert, your next goal. Your opponent has made a good choice of openings, but to paraphrase Siegbert Tarrasch, "After the opening, the gods have placed the middle game."

If you have bad experiences with the BCG, you might consider 2. Nf3. Players with a propensity to bookkeeping might note what openings they tend to win and lose. Those openings that give you bad results should be looked at carefully to see if a change might be desired.

4. cxb5 a6 5. e3

Class A players should find openings true to their style. For this reason we recommend 5. Nc3 axb5 6. e4. Most of your opponents will try 6. ..., b4 7. Nb5 Nxe4? 8. Qe2 winning (check it out!) and after 7. ..., d6 8. Nf3 the e-Pawn is still tainted: 8. ..., Nxe4 9. Bc4 g6 10. Qe2 Nf6 11. Bf4 and you should be happy.

The idea is to strive to make your opponent play your brand of chess. The move 5. e3 is Master play, but that is not always suitable to the Class A player.

5. ..., axb5 6. Bxb5 Ba6 7. Bxa6 Rxa6

OK, you have your extra Pawn. How do you intend to use it?

8. Nc3

The Class A player is not about to conceive a plan to use the a-Pawn. First development, king safety, then we will see about the a-Pawn. This is healthy Class A play.

8. ..., d6 9. Nf3 Nbd7 10. 0-0 g6
11. Qe2 Ra7 12. e4 Bg7 13. a4 (94)

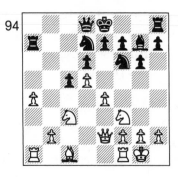

The lure of the new Queen! You have played the opening quite well. You even have established a central advantage. With 13. e5! you would increase that advantage. As a Class A player, you must be willing to fight in the center whenever you can. Study this position and decide for yourself how 13. e5! gives White the advantage.

What's wrong with 13. a4 ? Absolutely nothing–it may be the strongest move on the board, but given a choice between wing action and center action, the Class A player is better off seeking center action: that's where the strength of his game lies.

13. ..., 0-0 14. Nd2

A well-known maneuver played in many Master games – but not in this exact position–whose idea is Nc4 to support e5, a move White could have played on Move 13. It is important to know the reasons behind Master moves.

14. ..., Qa8 15. Nc4 Rb8

Your opponent is setting up the standard piece set up in the Benko. Notice how the Queen on a8 now makes e5 difficult.

16. Ra3 Ne8 17. Nb5? (95)

166

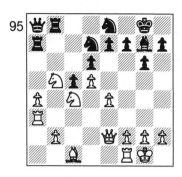

The problem of blunders is a spectre that haunts all levels of chess players. True, the stronger players experience them less. That does not comfort the player who makes an obvious error. You have just chucked the a-Pawn by this move which has a superficial appeal of occupying important queenside squares. We will not dwell on *why* the blunder occurs. We need to discuss the Class A player's attitude after the blunder.

17. ..., Rxa4

At this point the tournament player realizes he has made an elementary blunder. Emotions usually run high at this point. Two hours plus struggle has been negated in a single move. What is the Class A aspirant to do? A lot depends on your basic psychological makeup. If you are the excitable type, you need to get up from the board, go get a drink of water. If there is no time pressure, ignore the clock. Talk to somebody. About anything: release some of the emotion of the realization of the blunder. When you come back, be prepared to dig in and analyse what is going on.

If you are more phlegmatic, it may be advisable not to leave the board. Gain a few moments to control your thoughts. Remember, your opponent has emotions, too. He is lower rated and only thinks he is winning...maybe.

He suspects your blunder may be a trap. Keep a poker face. Be mentally tough: make your opponent work to capitalize on the blunder.

Alexander Pope said: Know thyself. There is no better advice to handle a blunder.

18. Qc2 Rxa3 19. Nbxa3 Ne5

Your reassessment of the position? The feeling after a blunder is that you are lost. As a student of this book, sitting in the relatively unemotional environment of your study, you can see that the position has lots of fight. Over-the-board, the situation can be different. You must remain true to your self. A French general expressed it best: "My flanks are collapsing, the center is decaying. What must I do? Attack! Always attack!" Your King is safe. Class B players are not known for their defensive ability. White must try 20. f4!? Why? Class A players are not great defenders either. Your chances are better attacking than defending. This is the attitude of the Class A player.

20. Bd2 Nxc4 21. Nxc4 Qa2

Notice how the non-attacking move 20. Bd2 is reducing White to passivity.

22. Rb1 Nc7 23. Bc1 Na6 (96)

The key to understanding what is going on is not so much the blunder, 17. Nb5, but White's play afterwards. Comment on White's play from Moves 18-23.

24. Na3 Nb4 25. Qc4 Qxc4 26. Nxc4 Nd3 27. Bg5

Now, in White's moment of desperation, you try aggressive moves. This is good Class A chess, but it is

too late.

27. ..., f6 28. Be3 f5 29. exf5 gxf5
30. Bg5 Kf7 31.b3 h6 32. Bh4 Nf4

And Black's threat of Ne2+ and Nd4 wins the b-Pawn. This is not accidental. Comment. Why is this happening to you?

33. Rd1 Rxb3 34. Kf1 Ng6

Because of White's passive attitude, horrible things are happening. The Class A player, analysing the game in his study (we always learn more from our losses) must understand what is going on. Review this game from move one if you do not know why you have such a bad game.

35. g3 Nxh4 36. gxh4 Bd4 37. Nd2 Ra3
38. Ke2 Ra2 39. Kf1 Bf6 40. h5 Ra1 (97)

Should you resign? No. Black still has problems to overcome. If you can save one game out of fifty by being stubborn, you have made a profit. This is a particularly odd stage of the game: time control has just been met. The actual time left on the clocks in this game is eight minutes for you, forty minutes for Black. Your opponent is in high spirits: he thinks he is winning. He is winning. But he must

still win the game.

**41. Rxa1 Bxa1 42.Nc4 f4 43. Ke2 Kf6
44. h4 Kf5 45. Kf3 Bf6 46. Nd2 Bxh4 47. Ne4 Bf6**

Zugzwang. Death is the hardest state to accept.

48. Nd2 Ke5 49. Ne4 Bg7

Good enough to win was 49. ..., Kxd5.

50. Nc3 Kf5 51. Nb5 Be5

Black's inaccurate, but winning, play illustrates why White should not resign such positions. Black may win 49 out of 50 such endings, but every once in awhile...

**52. Nc7 Kg5 53.Ne6+ Kxh5 54. Nxf4 Bxf4
55. Kxf4 Kg6 56. Ke4 h5 White Resigns**

You fought the good fight. You must never underestimate your opponent. Occasionally they will beat you; that is the nature of chess. The important thing is that you analyze your losses and learn from them. Chess without learning is no progress. Go back over this game. Find out not only where you went wrong, but why, if possible. Next time you will be prepared.

31. ENGLISH OPENING
White: 1685 Player
Black: You

1. c4 Nf6 2. Nc3 c5 3. Nf3 d5 4. cxd5 Nxd5 5. Nxd5

Comment on this move. Do not read the next sentence without first verbalizing what advantages or disadvantages lie in 5. Nxd5.

You must first realize that 5. Nxd5 is not favorable for White. It develops Black's Queen to a square where it influences the center. It prematurely reduces the center tension–after 5. g3, Black usually plays the retreat 5. ..., Nc7 or the exchange 5. ..., Nxc3, strengthening White's center.

If you listed as an advantage that it takes Black out of book, go back to the start of this book and begin to read it all over again. It won't hurt!

An excusable advantage is that it will bring the Black Queen on the diagonal of the white-squared Bishop. While this is true, the lessening of pressure on Black's game is more than ample compensation.

5. ..., Qxd5 6. g3 Nc6 7. Bg2 g6

This is well thought out by the Class A player (you)– you intend to pressure the d4 square and use the half-open d-file. Notice how playing this formation gives both your Bishops healthy diagonals (g7-b2 and c8-h3). The Knight on c6 fights for e5 and d4, and the Queen, for now, is well-posted.

This reflects the idea of seeking the maximum mobility and effectiveness of your pieces. After 7. ..., e5 8. 0-0 Be7, notice how much less effective the Bishop on e7 is. This noticing of such details is one of the hallmarks of the Class A player over the Class B player. It is *why* Class A players make better attackers than Class B players.

If you selected 7. ..., e5, don't worry. This is also a Class A play. An Expert is much more likely to choose ..., g6 over ..., e5.

8. 0-0 Bg7 9. d3 Qh5

The Queen did not have to vacate the center yet. Perfectly good was 9. ..., 0-0, but Black is in a hurry to begin his attack. This is a little premature, perhaps, but not a bad move.

A diversion: what books can a player serious enough to study books use to improve his play? The Class A aspirant might give some serious study to books about (or by) the old-time players. A study of Morphy and Steinitz can be very helpful. Morphy was the exponent of the open game. His opponents made errors very much in the style of modern Experts. Steinitz began the formulation of positional principles that every Class A player today should have a passing familiarity with. Studying the games and annotations of these old Masters games won't help your opening play any, but the games should shed some bright light on planning and preparing your middle game plans.

They were also both very good tacticians which should help the Class A player a lot.

10. Qb3 0-0 11. Bd2 Rb8

This is a nice move. Why? Black secures his base (b7), frees his white-squared Bishop for kingside activity, and allows his b-Pawn to advance to either b5 or b6 without worrying about the pin of the Knight on c6. There is also the possibility of ...Bb7 (after the b-Pawn moves) when the long diagonal is contested by a guarded Bishop. All-in-all, the player who understands the position well enough to play ..., Rb8 *should* be a Class A player.

12. Bc3 e5 (98)

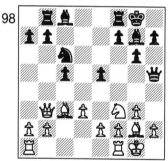

Comment upon this move. Does it make the g7 Bishop "bad"? Should Black have exchanged on c3 ? Is ..., e5 attacking or defensive ?

The Bishop on g7 may be a touch "worse," but it is not "bad" until the Pawn structure becomes locked. This

173

implies e4 by White which would leave the d-Pawn very anemic and the dangerous hole on d4. Consequently, White is unlikely to lock the e-Pawns.

To exchange on c3 would greatly ease White's game. The Pawn on c5 will soon need tending to; White will capture with the b-Pawn, strengthening his recessed center and inaugurating queenside pressure on the b-file to be followed by a4-a5, etc.

The move ..., e5 further pressures d4 (thematic, remember?) and prepares ..., Nd4 and ..., f5. Black has won the battle of the opening with 12. ..., e5.

13. e3?!

White, who has been playing "positional" chess, slips. This is because strategical openings such as the English are much more difficult to play than open games. Up to Class A strength players should learn the open game first. Then, as their strength has grown, they should branch out to closed systems. Ontogeny recapitulates phylogeny: this process of learning gives you the best base to learn the game of chess.

What is the flaw behind 13. e3?

13. ..., Bg4

Of course, the White center has been fatally weakened, and the d-Pawn is doomed. The Class B player has played to remove the pressure on d4 without considering the long-term effects. This is a common fault, as we have seen.

14. Nd2

Prove to yourself that 14. Qd1 loses a piece.

14. ..., Be2

If you found 14. Qd1 e4! 15. dxe4 Bxc3 16. bxc3 Ne5 you have a firm grasp on Class A tactics. If you found 16. h3! you are tactically gifted and should make Expert in little time.

15. Rfe1 Bxd3 16. Bxc6?!

Your opponent has become desperate. You know he is not in a good frame of mind because he missed his chance to get back in the game with 16. Qd5! What is your best bet to capitalize on his disorganized state of mind? The answer is very simple: forget psychology, make good chess moves. The weakness on White's kingside may not be immediately exploitable, but the time will come. Until then, Black will have to use his pieces aggressively, taking special care of his white-squared Bishop.

16. ..., bxc6 17. Qa3 c4 18. Qxa7

White has kept material equality. What is your short-range plan here? Long range?

18. ..., Rfe8

The aggressive Class A Candidate should be interested in getting rid of the piece that best defends White's light squares: the Knight on d2. With this piece gone, the squares h3 and f3 send out invitations to Black's Queen and Bishop: come, join the mate!

For this reason, Black should select the move 18. ..., Rfd8 (open file!) and watch how the game further develops.

19. Qc5 Rbc8 20. Nxc4?!

With the King Rook on d8, Black would already have
20. ..., Be4! but you have set up a clever defensive strategy.
This is good Class A play–setting traps or attacking: both
mean you are planning ahead.

20. ..., Bf8 21. Nd6 Rcd8? (99)

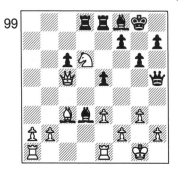

This is an error. Why? Correct was 21. ..., Red8 22.
Bxe5 Rxd6! 23. Bxd6 Qxc5 24. Bxc5 Bxc5 when Black has
a slight, but real, endgame advantage.

22. Qxc6?

White misses a win: 22. Nxe8! Why? Because he
believes he is losing. Why does he believe he is losing?
Because of Black's consistently aggressive play. This is
part of the bonus of pressuring your opponent. Class A
players benefit from such errors much more than their
lesser rated opponents. It may spoil the aesthetics of a
game to discover you allowed your opponent a win in a
difficult struggle, but perfect chess is not yet in the province
of man or machine. Winning chess, however, is another
story. This comes from the will to win, and the will to win
means pressuring your opponent until his will sags. You
will lose a few games by tactical accidents, but you will win
many more by adopting the aggressive stance of the Class
A player.

22. ..., Bxd6 23. Ba5

OK, what do we do now?

23. ..., Ra8! 24. Rad1

White sees that 24. Qxd6 is met by 24. ..., Be4! and Black will have time for either ..., Rxa5 or ..., Qf3 or both. The weakness of the white squares comes back, not mysteriously, not accidentally, but as a logical consequence of 16. ..., Bxc6.

24. ..., e4 25. Bc3 Be5

A new phase of the game: Black has an extra piece against two queenside Pawns. Since they haven't even thought of advancing to this time, Black should have no difficulties winning them, especially as White has to keep a constant eye on his weak kingside.

26. Rc1 Bxc3 27. Rxc3 Be2!

Notice Black's choice: play against the queenside Pawns or White's kingside. Comment.

28. Qf6 Bf3 29. Rc7 Rf8 30. h4

As 30. Qh4 is no way to play on, White plays on to answer 30. ..., Qg4 with 31. Kh2. What is your plan to continue? Analyse.

30. ..., Rad8?!

Black is of the opinion that anything will do. This is a dangerous attitude and has let many a game slip away. The correct idea is that the endgame is won for Black so he should challenge White's most aggressive piece by 30. ...,

Rac8! 31. R1c1 Rxc7 32. Rxc7 Qa5! and White has to allow the exchange of Queens or go over to pure defense. This is high class play but well within the scope of Class A players.

31. Qe7?

White could make Black's win much tougher with 31. Rxf7!

There is a lesson to be learned here, too. If you are going to resist in a patently lost position, then *resist.* To simply make moves in the hopes of dragging out the game to its inevitable end is a waste of your time. You must have the attitude that you will pounce on any mistake, no matter how small, that will strengthen your chances of survival. You must expect these errors, else how can you turn it around? This is a healthy Class A attitude in lost positions. It is not the attitude of the typical Class B player.

31. ..., Rd2 32. Rd7

See White's plan? To swap Rooks in a still losing position: this is minimal resistance.

32. ..., Qg4! White Resigns.

32. ENGLISH OPENING
White: 1485 Player
Black: You

1. Nf3

As a Class A player, you will still have plenty of opportunities to play Class C players. Should your attitude change? It probably should. You should be more intent on winning quickly and efficiently. Try to play a "nice" game, one that is, perhaps, publishable by your state chess association.

Should you experiment with different chess openings playing someone perhaps 400 rating points or more below you? Yes, definitely–but be sure your opening is *prepared,* one that you have been studying and would like to play. Don't just play something different for difference's sake. That is one sure way to find yourself in hot water in the opening. Playing the Class C player (or lower) is not a sure point on the scoreboard. The lowly "fish" has a nasty habit of biting one's ego, and sometimes biting hard. Play chess, Class A chess, and you will score the point.

1. ..., Nc6

This is playing something different for the sake of difference if Black is not prepared for 2. d4. Then after 2. ..., d5 3. c4, Black should have studied some of the major ideas of the Tchigorin Defense or he may find himself in a stew. If Black is ready for this, then 1. ..., Nc6 is perfectly good.

2. c4

The Class C player seeks safety. He does not have the fighting courage of a Class A player nor the knowledge of the Class B player. Generally the Class C player wants to avoid the fight with the Class A player. You should not give him that chance. Yes, you will outplay your opponent in the "fightless" game, but you will win sooner and more efficiently when you engage him in combat.

2. ..., e5

Into the center!

3. d3 f5

Also good is 3. ..., Nf6, but with 3. ..., f5, Black sets up an aggressive center formation. In Master play, this may not be best, but your opponent is a few rating points shy of that rank. This is not to suggest you should play inferior moves in the opening. You experimented a bit; after the game, you will study the opening and decide if you would like to experiment with this line again.

4. Nc3 Be7 5. Qc2 (100)

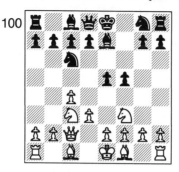

Criticize this move. Remember, not too long ago you were Class C strength. As a Class A player, would you consider 5. Qc2 ? If you rejected 5. Qc2 as premature–that White should locate his Bishop on f1 before placing his Queen, you have long ago moved out of Class C. Now, as a Class A player, how can you take advantage of White's misplaced Queen?

5. ..., Nf6

You, of course, realize that 5. ..., Nb4 is equally premature. Before you can punish Qc2 you must develop your kingside, castle, and see about opening up the center. The move 5. Qc2 is only premature, not bad. It offers no immediate refutation: its flaw is that many alternative placements of White's Bishop will be denied to him whereas 5. Qc2 puts so little pressure on Black's position, he may develop as he sees fit.

6. Bd2

Modesty, conserative play–all in accord with White's desire to avoid direct conflict. The Class A player should know that such positions are not easily conquered by storm. Most Class A players know the club player who opens up with 1. ..., a6 and 2. ..., h6 and then develops tenaciously, leaving himself a cramped position with no (or few) weaknesses. These players are hard to beat in the opening stage of the game. Patience and steady, sound chess will take their toll.

6. ..., 0-0 7. 0-0-0 d5

Black has played logically and feels it is time to open up the game. Analyse 8. cxd5 Nxd5 9. Nxd5 Qxd5 10. Qc4.

8. cxd5 Nd4

If you analysed (without moving the pieces!) 8. ..., Nxd5 9. Nxd5 Qxd5 10. Qc4 Qxc4+ 11. dxc4 e4 12. Ne1 Be6 13. e3 Bf6 as an ending favorable to Black, excellent! This is a favorable ending, do you wish to duck the ending for the middle game? This is not a bad choice. The Master would select the ending as being nearly won. The Class A player needs to be inventive. Attack is the soul of the Class A player.

9. Nxd4 exd4 10. Nb5 c5

Black sees that 10. ..., Qxd5 11. Qc4 Be6 fails to 12. Nxc7. He must change his original intent. He finds the tactical justification of 10. ..., c5. Did you? Analyse 11. dxc6 bxc6 12. Qxc6. How can Black win. You *must* find 12. ..., Bd7 13. Qa6 Qc8+! 14. Qxc8 Rxc8+ and ..., Bxb5. If you don't see this line, play it over again. Learn to see these lines mentally: it is the greatest asset to a Class A player.

11. Qb3 Rf7 12. d6 Bxd6 13. Nxd6 Qxd6 (101)

White has achieved the feared two Bishops, but what Bishops! One has no moves, the other has three safe squares to move to, two squares of which are worse than the square it is on. Black obviously has an edge. Note how

182

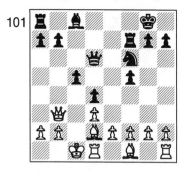

this happened: steady aggressive play.

14. Kb1 Be6 15. Qa3 b5

Does Black's attack play itself? Never! While it is true that an overwhelming Black force is concentrating itself on White's King, the Class A player must direct the attack. Are you ready? Let us watch this Class A player in attack and critique.

16. b4

Once again, the Class C player seeks to avoid battle, but we know what has happened here. He is weakening the side that is being attacked by moving Pawns in that arena. You must take advantage of this violation of general principles.

16. ..., c4 17. g3 Bd5

These moves are no accident, of course. Black's superior mobility prevent any easy development by White.

18. Bf4 Qe7 19. f3 a5!

Isn't chess fun? It should be. The Class A player has fun when he is attacking.

183

20. dxc4 axb4 21. Qc1 Ne4! (102)

There is an important principle behind this move: attack with all you've got!

22. fxe4 Bxe4+ 23. Rd3 Bxh1

An intermezzo: the Class A player takes the material; the rest of the attack will soon come back. A Class A player who is feeling his oats would have tried 23. ..., Rc8 or 23. ..., Qe6 or 23. ..., Qa7! all of which strongly continue the attack. Should Black take the material in a Class A versus Class C contest? No. Play aggressive chess, "beautiful" chess–it will pay off in the long run by making you a stronger player. True, the "1" on the tournament wall chart looks the same, but what you learn about chess is very different. The Rook on h1 has little to do with the game.

24. Rxd4 Be4+ 25. Kb2 Rxa2+!

Did this come as a surprise to you? It shouldn't. The Soviet Master Sokolov said he always approached the position on the board by asking himself, "What can I sacrifice now?" That's not a bad attitude!

26. Kb3

Simple analysis: what happens on 26. Kxa2?

26. ..., Qa7

Of course, even your Class D player will see the mate after 26. Kxa2, but the Class A player should now play 26. ..., Ra3+ 27. Kb2 Rc3 and White is doomed. White is still doomed now, but he can resist a bit by...

27. Rd8+ Rf8 28. Rxf8+ Kxf8
29. Bd6+ Ke8 30. Kxb4 Qa5+ 31. Kc5

Of course, 31. Kb3 Qa4+ 32. Kc3 Qxc4 mate is no fun for White; whether it is better, we'll leave to the philosophers.

31. ..., bxc4+ 32. Kd4 Qd5+ 33. Ke3 Qxd6

'Nuff said.

34. Qxc4 Ra3+ 35. Kf2 Qb6+ 36. e3 Qxe3 mate.

33. LARSEN'S OPENING
White: 1485 Player
Black: You

1. b3

OK, here is another one of those Class C players. You'd like to eat him up, of course. Let us critique Black's play.

1. ..., e5

This is a good line against the Larsen opening: center play and development, the two classic pillars of opening play.

2. e3 d5 3. Bb2 Bd6 4. c4 Nf6!?

This offers White an opportunity to "win" the e-Pawn for the c-Pawn by 5. c5 Bxc5 6. Bxe5 but after 6. ..., 0-0 7. Nf3 Nc6 Black has several tempi for the exchange and stands well.

5. Nf3 e4 6. Nd4 a6

Criticize this move. Why is it not a Class A move? What is better? More in keeping with Class A play is 6. ..., 0-0—let White waste time going after the Bishop on d6–6. ..., 0-0 7 Nb5? Nc6 8. Nxd6 Qxd6 and Black has too large a lead in development.

7. cxd5 Nxd5 8. Nc3 Nf6?!

Black retreats and loses time. This is not strong Class A play. After 8. ..., Nxc3 9. dxc3!? 0-0 the game is even.

9. d3!

The happiest point of Black's game was his e4 Pawn. Now this is disappearing and White has a lead in development, too. The Class A player–that's you–better dig in and find a method of handling White's position.

9. ..., c5 10. Nc2 Bg4 11. Be2 Bxe2 12. Qxe2 Be5?!

Black elected to simplify, but notice how he has developed White's game even more. Now he violates another opening tenet by moving a previously developed piece. Better was 12. ..., exd3 13. Qxd3 which brings the Queen to an exposed position and sets up the cheapo by 13. ..., 0-0 14. 0-0? Bxh2+!

13. 0-0-0!?

Your opponent is playing like a Class A player. You *must* dig in and find a line to survive here. We said we would critique Black's play. How would you evaluate 13. ..., Nc6 and 13. ..., 0-0 ?

13. ..., exd3

Black has a hard time here. The two moves he would

like to make, listed above, lose the e-Pawn with a good game for White. This disappointing choice happens because of Black's lackadaisical play in the opening. You cannot treat a Class C player cavalierly, or he will defeat you. You should not be overly concerned with the rating of your opponent. Being rated 400+ points above him does not guarantee success.

14. Rxd3 N8d7 15. R1d1 (103)

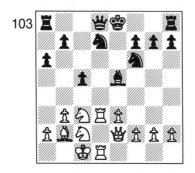

White has played very well, but Black has no weaknesses. There is no reason Black should lose this game. Yet. But Class A players were born to attack, and Black is not going to find much of a chance to attack for awhile yet. This means he will have to defend, and this is much harder for the Class A player to do.

15. ..., Qc7?!

Black must be very careful in such positions. Here he errs. Why is 15. ..., Qc7 weaker than 15. ..., Qe7 ? Note how the Bishop is shut out of a retreat by ..., Qc7 and this means the square d6 is weakened. Black should try 15. ..., 0-0.

16. g4!

Watch out—the threat is 17. g5 winning a piece. How should Black best react to this threat?

16. ..., h6?!

Black should have played 16. ..., 0-0-0 (catching up in development, relative king safety, in short–fighting!) 17. g5 Bxc3 18. Bxc3 Ne4! 19. Bxg7 Rhg8 and Black is fully in the game. Notice the attitudinal difference: on 16. ..., h6? Black is just defending against a White threat. On 16. ..., 0-0-0, Black is fighting, which is how Class A players should play.

17. f4 Bxc3 18. Rxc3

White avoids 18. Bxc3 as he fears 18. ..., c4 disrupting his position. This is a Class C reaction: fear. The Class A player would analyse 18. Bxc3 c4?! 19. bxc Qxc4 and find 20. Bxf6! gxf6 (why not 20. ..., Nxf6? You must see it!) 21. Qd2! and White's attack is a killer. So you have been given a respite. This will happen. In these battles there are often ebbs and flows. You must take advantage of your opponent when his will slackens.

18. ..., 0-0-0

Black would have liked to castle kingside to increase his fighting chances, but that short-sighted 16. ..., h6 means 18. ..., 0-0 19. g5! lets White's attack get there first. You should analyse the attacking and defensive lines for yourself (after all, in a tournament game no one is telling you how to win). Convince yourself if White can win or not.

19. Nd4 Ne4 20. Rc2 Rhe8 21. b4

White's play now should be encouraging to you. This attack is very two-edged, exposing his own King more than Black's. Formulate a plan. Don't move the pieces.

21. ..., Kb8

This is the proper start: the King is taken off the dangerous file.

22. Nb3 Rc8

This is another Class A play–the c-file is to be contested. Notice White's King is at the other end of this file.

23. bxc5 (104)

23. ..., Ka8?

What did Black see? The loss of an exchange after 23. ..., N/7xc5 24. Nxc5 Nxc5 25. Be5. And he stopped there. But after 25. ..., Rxe5! 26. fxe5 Qxe5, Black has a Pawn for the exchange and active pieces while White's Pawn structure is weak and his attack is gone. Should a Class A player be expected to see all this? Probably not, but this is the line he should play into: his whole game is set up for this. To play otherwise is to court disaster. Remember, this was part of Black's plan–all his pieces are set up to play this way. If he doesn't, his pieces are certain to be poorly posted for what happens next.

24. c6!

Nicely played–Class C players can attack, too. Black is facing severe threats now.

24. ..., bxc6?

Black has become discouraged in the last few plays as the game has not been going his way. This discouragement is a terrible enemy to the Class A player. You must learn to fight it off, if possible. This defeated attitude makes a Class A player play Class C chess. If Black could have shaken off the woes, he might have found 24. ..., N7f6 25. cxb+ Qxb7 with some chances to fight.

25. Qxa6+ Kb8 26. Bd4 c5 27. Rd3

Troubles come fast in this game. Notice what happens next.

27. ..., cxd4?!

Why does Black commit suicide in this position? He has allowed his will to be broken. He is a beaten man. You must find ways of strengthening this will. How you do it is up to you, but it must be done if you are to improve steadily, else you must expect setbacks.

28. Rxc7 Rxc7+ 29. Kb2 N7c5 30. Qb5+ Ka7 31. Nxc5 Rb8 32. Ra3 mate.

These are the games that make you stronger: the painful losses. They should be carefully studied. It is not enough, for example, to decide that 6. ..., 0-0 is a better move than 6. ..., a6. You must understand why it is a better move and plan to incorporate this general information into your chess playing. It is not enough to find a defense in a particular position, 16. ..., h6? You must find an active defense and understand why it is better (in general). Then the goal of Class A player is in your grasp.

34. QUEEN'S GAMBIT DECLINED
White: You
Black: 2105 Player

1. d4 d5 2. c4 e6 3. Nc3 c5

Now you as a Class A player are given a stern test. The Expert you are playing wants to beat you. He has selected the Tarrasch Defense where the isolated d-Pawn has elements of strength and weakness. If you do not handle the isolani well, it will expand and rough you up.

4. cxd5 exd5 5. Nf3 Nc6 6. g3

This is Rubinstein's move. Rubinstein was a Grandmaster, and he played this move with a Grandmaster's understanding of the position. As a Class A player you may have memorized this sequence. Do you understand why Rubinstein played 6. g3? The Class A level is the level where the understanding of opening play begins to deepen. Buy a book on the Tarrasch Defense. Find out why 6. g3 is played. It will deepen your understanding of the game.

6. ..., Nf6 7. Bg2 Be7 8. 0-0 0-0 9. dxc5 Bxc5 (105)

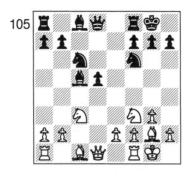

We have here the standard Tarrasch setup. Black has an isolated Pawn. Why is it weak? It cannot be protected by another Pawn. It does not exercise control over the square immediately in front of it (d4). Why is it strong? It controls two squares in White's territory, c4 and the center square e4. If the Pawn advances it may have a cramping influence on White's game.

What then is White's plan?

10. Na4

This is White's plan, to secure control of d4 to prevent White from advancing.

10. ..., Be7 11. Be3 Re8 12. h3?

This does not fit well into White's plan. The square c5 is weak, too. After 12. Rc1 (open file) White need not fear 12. ..., Ng4 13. Bc5 Bxc5 14. Nxc5 and White can blockade the d-Pawn on d4 or d3.

12. ..., Ne4

Black follows his game plan–active minor pieces will compensate for the weakness on d5: the center is coming under Black control.

13. Nd4 Bd7

Black correctly refrains from 13. ..., Nxd4 14. Bxd4 Bf6 as exchanges are not favorable to the side with the isolani. Piece activity lessens as pieces are removed from the board.

14. Rc1 Qa5 15. Nc3

White is forced backwards by the threat of ..., Nxd4. This move incorporates a Pawn sacrifice. Can Black take it?

15. ..., Bf6?!

Black elects to continue the pressure on White's center, but he could have cashed in by 15. ..., Nxc3 16. Rxc3 Qxa2 17. Qc2 Rac8 with a Pawn plus. Why does the Expert allow this opportunity to escape? The answer is simple: Experts are only a little stronger than you. You don't see it all, either (no one does!). The Expert is afraid of White's counterplay against d5, but he shouldn't be. Black's decision to avoid complications is uncharacteristic of Expert play, but you as a Class A player must have some breaks if you are to beat an Expert.

16. Nb3

Now the d-Pawn seems doomed. Analyse what is about to occur. Don't move the pieces.

16. ..., Nxc3 17. Nxa5 Nxd1 18. Rfxd1 Bxb2
19. Rc2 d4 20. Rxb2 Nxa5 21. Rxd4 (106)

The complications are over. The Expert's failure to punish your opening play has rebounded to his disadvantage. What would you think of offering a draw in this position? Remember your opponent is rated 2105.

21. ..., Bc6

White, to his credit, did not offer a draw here. Nevertheless, a draw would not be an unreasonable outcome in this position. White has the advantage, but Black has counterplay. If your opponent takes the draw, OK. If not, you will learn much about such endings.

22. Bxc6 Nxc6 23. Rd7 b6 24. Rc2 Re7 25. R2d2

White keeps a bind on the position this way. Premature, of course, is 25. Rxe7 Nxe7 26. Rc7? Nd5 with the advantage.

25. ..., Kf8 26. Bg5 f6 27. Bf4 Ke8 28. R7d6

Notice how White rejects the exchange of Rooks–good play! White's Rooks are stronger than Black's (more active). White's reasoning can be based on Pawn structure. If all the pieces are off the board, Black wins. Therefore, each exchange would bring Black closer to that goal. White declines to exchange. This is good Class A thinking.

28. ..., Rc8? (107)

29. Rc2!

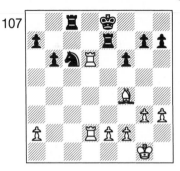

Black's error was not entirely accidental. White encouraged the error by his strong play. The Class A player can learn from this: attack, attack, always attack. If the Class A player is true to this philosophy, he will soon find his rating increasing.

29. ..., R7c7 30. Re6+ Kd7 31. Re3 Rb7 32. Rd3+?

You have already worked out 32. Rd2+ and wins. Our Class A player has not. Why not when it is so obvious to you and me? It is because he isn't looking for it. He has let the Expert's rating hypnotize him. Who, little old me win? Don't be silly. It's just a matter of time before he beats me but I'll give it the old college try.

Hogwash! but true. Many players are beaten before they begin play. Our Class A player has been playing very well, but now he falters, temporarily. It will happen to you too. These setbacks will become less and less as your rating increases, or perhaps it's as these setbacks decrease, your rating increases.

There is little doubt if the opponent were rated 1405, White would have found 32. Rd2+ in a flash.

32. ..., Ke8 33. Rdc3 Kd7 34. Rd2+ Ke8
35. R2c2 Kd7 36. h4!

Having demonstrated to himself Black's helplessness to refuse the draw, White gains in courage. He knows the Expert wants the draw, has nothing more than a draw, and so now, with new found courage, can play for the win.

36. ..., a6?!

Black might have tried 36. ..., Ne7 immediately, but he feels he has to get his queenside moving.

37. Kg2 Ne7 38. Rd3+ Ke8
39. R2d2 Nc6 40. Rd6 Ne7 41. e4

White has made a little progress since he spurned the draw: his kingside Pawns are advancing and Black's are several moves behind and not likely to move for awhile yet.

41. ..., Ng6 42. Re6+

White's decision to go after Black's queenside Pawns shows the confidence gained by the Class A player. Bravo! If you can play like this, you are on your way to an Expert's rating! White has all the chances to win.

42. ..., Kf7 43. R2d6! Nxf4+ 44. gxf4 Rc2!

This enables Black to hold the game, but the Class A player still holds the reins.

45. a4 Ra2 46. Rxb6 Rxb6 47. Rxb6 Rxa4
48. Kf3 a5 49. h5

This locks the King to the kingside and White is certain of at least a draw. The Class A player played resolutely in this game, not allowing the Expert to push him around. But the game is not over yet. The Expert will try everything he can to try to win this position. You must be up to resist his will.

**49. ..., h6 50. Ra6 Ra1 51. Kg4 a4
52. Kf5 a3 53. Ra7+ Kg8 54. e5 fxe5
55. fxe5 a2 56. f4 Rh1?**

Sometimes the Expert can try too hard–can you find a White win?

57. Rxa2 Rxh5+? 58. Kg6 Black Resigns

This was, despite the error on Move 32, a fine game by the Class A player. He put pressure on Black throughout the game. Experts can be had. As a Class A player, they are your next goal. A good book for you might be *How To Become a Candidate Master*, the next volume in this series.

35. SICILIAN DEFENSE
White: You
Black: 2176 Player

1. e4 c5 2. Nf3 d6 3. d4 cxd4 4. Nxd4 Nf6 5. Nc3 g6

The Expert has selected the Dragon Variation of the Sicilian. This means he intends to attack you with all his pieces. What is the best choice for the Class A player, 6. Be2 or 6. Bc4 ?

6. Be2

If the Class A player is facing another Class A player or lower rated player, this move can hardly be faulted. Playing someone substantially higher rated, however, it is necessary to constantly pressure your opponent. For this reason, the sharper 6. Bc4 is the move. You may be mated quicker, but you may also scale the Dragon and take the Expert's hide.

What if you don't "know" the 6. Bc4 line but are familiar with the lines from 6. Be2 ? Should you try the new line or stick with old safe-n-sane? The answer may depend on your temperament, but generally you are better off playing known lines. Let your higher-rated opponent vary first from book: you'll have a better chance to get an advantage from the opening in that way. *But,* make a mental note to learn the lines that evolve from 6. Bc4. The next time it comes up, try your wings.

6. ..., Bg7 7. 0-0 0-0 8. Be3 Nc6 9. a4

Evaluate this move. Does it fit into White's piece and Pawn configuration. Does it affect Black's configuration?

This move is usually played to prevent Black's queenside expansion with ..., a6 and ..., b5. As Black has not made a move toward this queenside growth, we can label 9. a4 as a wasted move. The Class A player who played 6. Be2 because he "knows" this line better than 6. Bc4 was fooling himself in this instance. It is too tough to play "positional" chess against a player rated too far above you. Tactical play offers many more opportunities to score a point, or even half a point.

9. ..., d5!?

The Expert knows the rule of Sicilians: if Black can attain ..., d5 safely in the opening, he has equalized. Now a lot of simplification occurs. Is this to the lower-rated player's advantage in that it will make life easier? No, because the tactical chances become very small and the Expert's greater understanding of the power of the remaining pieces will make him a heavy favorite.

10. exd5 Nxd5 11. Nxd5 Nxd4 12. Bxd4

Why can White not win a Pawn by 12. Nxe7+? Analyse.

12. ..., Qxd5 13. Bxg7 Qxd1

14. Rfxd1 Kxg7 15. Bf3 Bf5 (108)

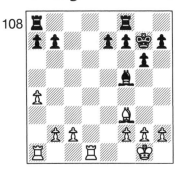

Evaluate the ending which has been reached. Who has the better chances? Which side would you prefer to play?

Objectively, White actually has the better chances here based on his superior development and queenside Pawn majority. Practically, the chances are about even. The Expert is happy because the position is unbalanced. He has a Pawn majority also and will know how to use it. Why is White's majority superior? Because a three to two majority will produce a passed Pawn faster than a four to three. The passed Pawn will then procede to cost the other side a piece. With the extra piece, the other side will win some Pawns on the other side, make a new Queen, and mate. That would be the ideal script if the Expert were playing White.

16. Bxb7?

The Class A player, on the other hand, does not understand the strength of his position and plays to establish the passed Pawn *immediately* and in the process allows Black's forces to become active. That activity will render the passed Pawn weaker until it becomes a target. Correct was 16. Rd2 or 16. c3.

16. ..., Rab8 17. Bf3 Rxb2 18. c4 Rc8 19. Rac1 Rc2!

It is instructive to watch the Expert's technique: he will use his superior development to catch the c-Pawn, and then his winning procedure will be as described above. The Class A player will not have the ending skills of the Expert but he can learn by analysing the game afterwards.

In the analysis afterwards, it is not enough for the Class A player to "blame" 9. a4 and 16. Bxb7. He must understand the attitude behind each move that made him choose these inferior moves.

20. g4 R8xc4! 21. Rxc2 Bxc2 22. Rcl Bb3 (109)

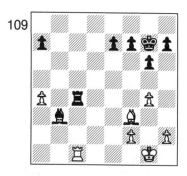

Should White exchange Rooks? Why or why not?

23. Rbl

This is the correct choice. The Rooks are needed to prevent Black from just walking through White's defenses as Black's King would get to the center and queenside too fast. White's Pawn on a4 is too easy a target. Verify this for yourself. Play the ending after 23. Rxc4 for yourself a few times. Get a feel for it. If you have a computer that accepts chess positions, play this position a few times against it.

23. ..., Bxa4 24. Rb7 a5 25. Rxe7 Bc6?!

Experts have problems with endings too. After 25. ...,

Bb3! the Bishop will support the advance of the a-Pawn, protect f7, and Black will push the a-Pawn to a2 and then the Rook on the first rank will allow the Pawn to catch a piece.

26. Bxc6 Rxc6 27. Ra7 Rc1+ 28. Kg2 Ra1 (110)

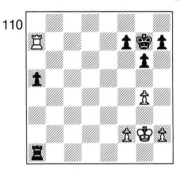

This is another position that separates the Class A player from the Expert. The Expert has studied endgames more than the Class A player. It is not enough to ask if this position is a win or a draw. You must know the plan for winning or drawing. This learning can be gained, but what endings should you study? There are too many endings to study all of them. If you want to improve, study the endings that arise in your games. After this game is over, analyse your game. Look up this kind of ending in *Basic Chess Endings* or some other book on endings. Learn the general plans of offense and defense. The next time this kind of ending appears in one of your games, you will be ready for it.

29. Ra6 a4 30. h4?!

One of the keys to most Rook and Pawn endings is how to handle the Pawns on the other side of the board. White will want to exchange off those Pawns to make defense easier, but White must wait until the Black King goes queenside. By advancing them while the King is on the kingside makes them targets to the Black King. White's King will be tied down to g2 and h2 to prevent Black's Rook from moving away with check from the a-Pawn.

30. ..., a3 31. f4? a2!

Now the White Rook is tied to the a-file, the White King to g2 and h2. What happens on 32. Kf2 ? Just 32. ..., Rh1!

32. h5

White continues to make it easy. He must study the course of this ending so he may handle it better next time or use the techniques learned to win the Black side in later games.

32. ..., gxh5 33. gxh5 h6 34. f5 f6 35. Kh2 Kf7
36. Kg2 Ke7 37. Kh2 Kd7 38. Kg2 Kc7
39. Kh2 Kb7 40. Ra3 Kb6 41. Kg2 Kc5 White Resigns

The win is clear: Black will wander with his King to g5, capture the h-Pawn, post his King on g4, advance the h-Pawn to h3 when White's King will have no moves, the White Rook will have to abandon the f-Pawn, which Black will capture with an easy win.

Endings can be logical, but tough! At the conclusion of a game like this, you should ask for a post mortem. Learn from your adversary. Many of his ideas may be valuable to you.

COLOPHON

This book was set in Cardinal. Typography by *typefaces, inc.* Cover Design by Reed Graphics.

Typesetting by Terry Pickett and Bob Long. Paste-up by Brian Smith. File handling from Dunne's disk Manuscript by Kathy Cooke.

Thinkers' Press
Catalogue

Thinkers' Press is known worldwide for its quality chess literature. We give new talent a chance if we think the goods are good!

Known also for our quick delivery and postpaid shipping of our products, we have decided to take on the product line of a few other entrepreneurs who believe in us as we believe in them. You can be assured of top notch materials because what we sell through this catalog is guaranteed or your money back.

The secret is in originality and fine production. Take a look on the next few pages and try something right now.

THE OPENING

Alekhine's Defense Four Pawns Attack: *GM Christiansen, Joseph, Raingruber, flexi*

This attack is probably the one Black fears most. Designed like the below King's Gambit book, we expect this book to arm White with a very strong weapon for his 1. e4 arsenal. *To be published at the end of 1987.* **$10.95 (tent.)**

The French Defense: *Nikolay Minev, flexi*

450 annotated games by one of the world's experts. Minev has been the editor-in-chief for the French section in *ECO.* This book delves into refuted, disputed, and improved lines with many new suggestions (1,000!).

The last 20 games display typical tactical tricks and sacrifices. Extremely up to date.

In our opinion, the best book ever produced on the French Defense. *To be published at end of 1987.* **$19.95 (tent.)**

The King's Gambit as White: *GM Christiansen, Maser, Raingruber, flexi*

Revised second edition. This book led the upsurge in popularity of the King's Gambit. The authors are proponents of the Kieseritzky and examine all attempts by Black to vary from this plan (such as Fischer's plan or the Falkbeer Countergambit).

Unlike many opening books, this is a textbook with problems and solutions at the end of each of the 16 chapters. Although the King's Gambit is often thought of as a tactical opening, this book takes a positional stance with emphatic play on winning with the White pieces. Published in 1986. **$14.95**

The Latvian Gambit: *Grivainis, flexi*

Popular among gambiteers, this opening is designed for the fearless and those that are looking for new ways to win. This games collection features nearly 800 entries from all the big events and the lesser known ones.

The greatest names in the business are here and the index for each variation will guide you through the entanglements. The book is loaded with evaluations and diagrams as well as light notes by a senior postal chess master.

There are more details on the Latvian Gambit in this book than any other published and it has been hailed for its currency of evaluations. History and introductions in 6 languages. Figurine algebraic notation. Published in 1985. **$17.95**

Romanishin Variation (4.g3) of the Nimzo-Indian Defense: *Spiro, flexi*
Spiro's capacity for hard work is demonstrated in this system against the fighting Nimzo-Indian. Was he a prophet? This system appeared twice in the Karpov-Kasparov WCC match.

Max Euwe, Dutch world champion, thought this might be the solution against the Nimzo-Indian and the difficult job of making sense out of all the transpositions from such openings as the English is handled deftly in the 3 chapters (4... c5, 4... d5, and seldom played). Published in 1981. **$5.00**

Bird's Defense to the Ruy Lopez: *McCormick, GM Soltis, hardcover*
A heady publication of a defense that Tarrasch claimed defied refutation and which Bronstein called an "attack" rather than a defense.
The system goes *1. P-K4 P-K4 2. N-KB3 N-QB3 3. B-KN5 N-Q5.* Over 200 games plus introductions each section are given. You can count on the thoroughness of the authors.
Published by McFarland & Company in 1981 and remaindered by *Thinkers' Press.* **$13.95**

The LDL Sicilian: *Dunne, flexi*
An 8 chapter dissertation on a "new" winning method against the Sicilian Defense (1 e4 c5 2 g3!?). Dunne presents many of his own games because the literature is virtually void. This is a Lasker suggestion. 30 pages to fit inside a business-size envelope. *Late 1987.* **$5.00**

The Sicilian Wing Gambit: *Hurt, flexi*
The author has played this White attacking system for years and scored many wins with it (over 60 of his lines are given here). Hurt is an eternal optimist and has extracted some materials from other sources and broken the book into the accepted, declined, and deferred.
Over 100 stem lines are given in *MCO* style format. Algebraic notation. Published in 1983. **$8.00**

The Anti-Indian Trompowski's Attack: *Savage, flexi*
Pawn formations, new games and strong analysis have made this a "must" book for those that want to infuse new life into their opening play. *1 d4 Nf6 2 Bg5* is explored in: 3 Bxf6, 2... Ne4, and 2... c5.
Savage's analysis has won praise from many masters. Each chapter is concluded with a summary. Published in 1984. **$9.00**

TREATISES

How to Be A Class A Player: *Dunne, flexi*
New this fall (1987). Another first rate study by Master Dunne on attaining an 1800-1999 rating by playing those within your target range. 35 games are penetratingly analysed from your level and tidbits are sprinkled everywhere to show you how to achieve the attitude of a winner.
According to many that bought Dunne's *How to Become a Candidate Master,* his approach works and works even better with each reading.
You'll be surprised how much you don't know. **$14.95 (tent.)**

How to Become a Candidate Master: *Dunne, flexi*
So popular a second and revised edition was necessary!
Most of us want to make "expert" and this book has 50 annotated games whose sole purpose is to get you to win more often and to tone up that killer instinct by informing you of what your opponents are thinking and doing.
A wide variety of openings are portrayed. The middle game, the stomping ground of the expert, and the endgame, the field of the master, are also cast to get you used to winning in *any* phase of the game.
Published in 1986. **$16.95**

Answer Guide to How to Become a Candidate Master: *Dunne, flexi*
This book came about because of the tremendous popularity of Dunne's book. Besides a biographical background of the author, there are answers to questions posed in Dunne's book, ratings of the combatants, and corrections to the first edition.
Published in 1986. **$3.95**

Practical Chess Analysis: *Buckley, flexi*
A brilliant expose of how masters analyze and how you can too. The methods and aims are illustrated through many fine examples. If you are tired of cliched games that have been used hundreds of times, you'll like this book because the author shows you how he did it.
The aims are to systematize the way you think so that you can carry a logical chain of reasoning in your head once you know what your aims are.
We think this is one of the best "middle game" type books to be published in years. *This fall (1987).* **$16.95 (tent.)**

Predicament in 2-Dimensions: *Mengarini, flexi*
This book produced a sensation when first published. GM Bisguier was extremely enthusiastic. Besides the 36 annotated games at the back, this book is a philosophical enhancement of what is going on in most chess players' minds because, you see, Mengarini is a psychiatrist with a Master's rating.
Blending physics, psychology, and some good old "common sense" school of hard knocks reality... this book carries a warning label: "This book was written to make you think!"
"I wish I had a reputation. It makes winning so matter-of-course."
"When two people sit down to a game, almost invariably one has a psychological advantage. It is more real and more deadly than rooks doubled on the seventh."
Now one of the classic books. Third printing published in 1982. **$8.50**

How to Reassess Your Chess: *Silman, flexi*
Our forte seems to be in improvement books and this is one of the best by test.
Each reading will improve your game because you discard your jumbled ideas about chess and evolve into a cohesive understanding of what chess really is.
Examples with students he has taught occupy 25 pages. This is the real measure of your "theory".
What you find out about Knights and Bishops and control of the center may be some of the most important information you will ever use. Silman's examples prove conclusively that chess is not an art form but a study of imbalance resulting in a scientific application of principles.
Published in 1986. **$14.95**

ENDGAME

Endgame Artillery: *Angos, flexi*
  Although there were less than 500 players at the 1982 US Open in St. Paul, we sold 30 copies of this book in less than 2 days! The majority of buyers were Masters and many of them told me this was a great book on a subject that had virtually no coverage in depth, Queens and Rooks.
  I was selling at a tournament in Milwaukee when a Queens and Rooks endgame appeared among two players rated over 2100. While they were floundering around Angos turns to me and says, "If they had read my book, this game would've been over a long time ago!"
  Master Angos is a professor and former player for the Greek Chess Olympic team. IM Bill Martz told me that Angos was of GM strength when it came to the endgame.
  Supplies are very limited. Published in 1982. **$12.95**

BIOGRAPHICAL

Salo Flohr's Best Games of Chess: *Donges, flexi*
  Reacting to a need for a book on Flohr, Thinkers' Press published Dr. Donges' book in 1985.
  While he was often compared to Capablanca in his technique (excellent endgame play, willing to take draws), he also could do some things on his own such as win at Hastings 5 times!
  His opening expertise was in the English and Caro-Kann (9 and 6 examples respectively, are included in this book) although he was no stranger to the Slav and many other QP systems.
  In the early 1930's Flohr, along with Alekhine, was probably the strongest player in the world. This book presents 50 games of "sound common sense" depicting his flawless positional judgment and his superb endgame technique. **$10.00**

Persona Non Grata: *Kortchnoi & Cavallaro, flexi*
  We published a book that received bad press! One reviewer mentioned that Kortchnoi was a communist (whether he was or not was irrelevant — Kortchnoi defected!). Others thought the book was written by Cavallaro. Not true! We had the original Russian manuscript but what Cavallaro did was take Kortchnoi's style and turn it into a readable manuscript plus he added some facts surrounding all the controversy about the world championship title. All of Kortchnoi's comments are typeset in italic.
  This book was originally called "Anti-Chess" when published in Europe but we had a number of things none of the other books had.
  For example, photos from Kortchnoi & Sztein's collection; 7 annotated games (3 by Kortchnoi, the other 4 by Alburt and Shamkovich) from the 1978 match where Kortchnoi almost pulled off the most unbelievable comeback in chess history; an afterwords, letters, and many other appended items (10 in all).
  Kortchnoi's notes to 3 games is easily worth the small price of this book.
  Published in 1981 during his match with Karpov. **$8.95**. There is also a very small supply of hardcover editions at **$20.00** or get both for **$25.00**

Grandmaster Fearless: *Long, flexi*
  This little pamphlet came on the heels (1982) of the above title.
Kortchnoi's results in USSR championships have never been equalled —
4 wins (27th, 30th, 32nd, and 38th).
  An article never before translated into English appears by David
Bronstein on Kortchnoi's winning the 27th.
  Kortchnoi told me in Chicago (1982), "Americans like to listen to chess.
They like to watch chess, but they don't like to read chess." Can you prove
him wrong?
  There are 13 games and 6 are annotated. Also included are Kortchnoi's
scores against the world champions (Karpov is the only player who has a
better percentage). This is a good addenda to the *Persona* book. **$2.00**

Viktors Pupols, American Master: *Parr, flexi*
  The author is now editor of *Chess Life* and the preface is by our top
player, Yasser Seirawan!
  One of the all time bargains of the century, this chess book is about a
player who probably feared no man and he mowed down a lot of talent.
Living in the NW part of the US, this Latvian has played the best (including
Fischer in a lot of skittles games where he pounded Bobby).
  If you are looking for some tactical chess, stop! We have a Benko, 10
Latvian Gambits, 12 Sicilians, a Two Knights... Strategical games? We have
them too, e.g.: 12 French Defenses, 12 Ruy Lopezes, and a lot more.
  Pupols was not boring by a long shot. He punched out old Jim
McCormick for being a nuisance, he rode in a cold contraption (car) on
the way back from a tournament that damn near killed him and his
number of tournament wins (95) is probably some kind of record.
  One special section of the book is 9 pages and it is on the theoretical
aspects of the play of "Unkel Vik". A great and entertaining chess book.
Includes photographs. **$6.50**

My Chess Adventures: *Warburton & Bogan, flexi*
  Some of the most interesting chess players I've ever been introduced to
were not GM's but guys like Charles Warburton.
  Warburton is crusty and he's often right. He has the ability to analyze to
perfection. He's played in British postal championships for decades and
been a best games judge numerous times as well as an adjudicator, a job
he took very seriously.
  The truth of chess will descend upon you. The Lopez is his favorite
weapon, whether from the White or Black side. He will show you special
treatments of "inferior" openings such as the Caro-Kann, the Sicilian, and
the English!
  You'll travel to the deserts of Africa and around the correspondence
globe. Some games will be miniatures in a devastating fashion and
others are brilliant struggles to 'prove a point'.
  The essays, analyses, and stories are a goldmine of talent and
observation.
  In descriptive notation, this book also includes photographs. Published
in 1984. **$14.95**

Lasker & His Contemporaries

In 1978 we began publishing a series about Emanuel Lasker and the Golden Age of chess. Edited by Bob Long, contributors have included Wolfgang Heidenfeld, C.J.S. Purdy, GM Larry Evans, Dr. Nathan Divinsky, Dale Brandreth and, of course, the main man himself, Lasker!

Translations, theories, photos, new articles, and some incredible game annotations cover Lasker and the other giants of chess. The fifth issue will cover Lasker's mathematical career, Steinitz, and much more.

An oasis in a Sahara of chess literature. All are 8½x11 format.

Issue One: Capablanca-Lasker negotiations, Lasker's profundity, the Earliest Recorded Lasker Game, Annotated Games, and the Ten Best Controversy. 36 pp. **$7.00**

Issue Two: The Great Steinitz Hoax, Karl Schlechter, 1903 Lasker-Chigorin, Lasker the Mathematician and the 1910 lectures in South America. 40 pp. **$7.00**

Issue Three: Lasker vs. the Devil, New York 1893, Frank Marshall, Chess & Strategy, Lasker's Forgotten Games, and Lasker in the USSR. 48 pp. **$8.00**

Issue Four: Doomsday Encounter, Khrulev on Lasker, Marshall and Lasker, Cambridge Springs, 1894 Match, Lasker's Visit to Spain, Chess Nerves and the Annotated Lasker. 56 pp. **$10.00**

The Lasker Poster: A beautiful, full size, two-color rendering of the artwork designed by Bob O'Hare for *Lasker & His Contemporaries.* Orange-brown and black. Great for framing. Sent in tube. Price includes shipping. **$6.95**

SOFTWARE

From Enlightenment Inc.:

Paul Whitehead Teaches Chess: *Apple II+ (64K), IIe, IIc, and IIGS; the Commodore 64/128; IBM PC (mono or color)*

Throw away your beginner books and a lot of books at the intermediate level because this software was designed to save you the trouble of rummaging through tons of paperwork.

There are two 2-sided diskettes encompassing dozens of topics from strategy to tactics. I don't think the author left anything out! The endgame section is very good.

Also included is IM Julio Kaplan's *Coffeehouse Chess Monster!* Thousands of these diskettes have been sold and the price for what you get is a real bargain! **$59.95**

50 (annotated) Classic Chess Games: *above systems*

This wonderful package contains two 2-sided diskettes that are jammed with annotated classics such as Lasker-Capablanca 1914. What makes this interesting is that you can actually see the moves progess (at your rate) through the game allowing you to guess(?) what would happen next. You can also go back to any position (and alternatives are also offered).

Boot up the disk and the instructions take you easily through the environment. Easy and enjoyable. **$19.95**

Jeremy Silman's Guide to Chess Openings: *above systems*
This is truly great! Not only is it a repertoire system but you are allowed many alternatives by your opponent and often there are comments at critical junctions.

In the bizarre replies section Silman thoughtfully unleashes moves that strangle and perforate your opponent — moves that often are not in the current opening books!

Also included, FREE, is Kaplan's *Coffeehouse Chess Monster.* From the White side the Lopez is recommended but he will take you through all of Black's side alleys such as the Sicilian, the French... If White opens with 1 d4 then Silman's customized reply will keep White off balance in most lines and actually make life miserable for the unprepared. I used this system recently, quite successfully.

There are three 2-sided diskettes included and a huge road map for you to follow where you've been and show you where you are headed. Silman is great on this. **$59.95**

Najdorf Sicilian Defense: *Ladow and Biyiasas, above systems*
Intensive and extensive analysis of the infamous Najdorf. The brochure says, "You can spring these lines on even the most advanced players" because Biyiasas has revealed new analysis not published elsewhere. That ought to whet your appetite!

The *Coffeehouse Chess Monster* is included (two diskette pkg.). You'll love this. **$39.95**

King's Indian Defense (4 e4 lines): *Chang and Biyiasas, above systems*
Again like the Najdorf disk, there is material on this popular system (3 diskettes) never published before. Again, the Kaplan *Coffeehouse Chess Monster* is included free of charge.

The instructions for use are easy. **$39.95**

VIDEOTAPE

CHESS: A Winner's Strategy: *Silman, Beta or VHS*
About one-half hour of great visuals, succinct learning aids, all in color. Professionally produced and geared towards supplementing Silman's *How to Reassess Your Chess* book.

The pieces magically move around the board to give you clues in new thinking techniques for all players. All the time there is the maestro speaking to you about what is happening. **$26.95**

If you order this tape in conjunction with the *How to Reassess Your Chess* book you can save considerably. Get both for **$37.90**

All Thinkers' Press Catalogue items are sent postpaid!

Visa and MasterCard are accepted. Phone: (319) 323-7117 and our answering machine (Clyde) will take your order.

THINKERS' PRESS
301 Union Arcade Building
Davenport, Iowa 52801